The
FINANCIALLY
CONFIDENT
WOMAN

*The Least Every Woman Needs to Know
to Manage Her Finances and Prepare for the Future*

FINANCIALLY
CONFIDENT
WOMAN

*The Least Every Woman Needs to Know
to Manage Her Finances and Prepare for the Future*

MARY HUNT

Founder and Publisher, Debt-Proof Living

DPL
PRESS

Los Angeles

Tiptionary, Live Your Life For Half The Price, Debt-Proof Living, Live the Plan!, Cheapskate Monthly, Rapid Debt-Repayment Plan, Rapid Debt-Repayment Plan Calculator, Freedom Account and Everyday Cheapskate are registered trademarks of Mary Hunt.

PRINTED IN THE UNITED STATES OF AMERICA

Cover Design: Jeremy Hunt, *SDMFX.com*

For information regarding special discounts for bulk purchases and or corporate branding, please contact:

DPL Press, Inc., P.O. Box 2135, Los Angeles, CA 90723;
Special Sales: 800-550-3502. Visit us at *DPLPress.com*.

First edition published 1996.

Library of Congress Cataloging-in-Publication Data
Information Available by Request from Publisher

ISBN-13: 978-1-934508-01-5

1   2   3   4   5   6   7   8   9   10

This book is lovingly dedicated to
Posy Lough
a confident woman
whom I am blessed to call my friend,
colleague and mentor.

Also by Mary Hunt

Debt-Proof The Holidays

Tiptionary 2

Debt-Proof Living - Revised and Updated

Live Your Life For Half The Price

Everyday Cheapskate's Greatest Tips

Debt-Proof Your Marriage

Debt-Proof Your Kids

Tiptionary

The Complete Cheapskate

Money Makeover

The Best of Cheapskate Monthly

Table of Contents

Introduction

I t was my junior year of high school, second semester. I was down to the wire and in desperate need of just one more elective to fill my class schedule. Any class that promised an easy "A" would do. Little did I know that my class decision would go on to become a defining moment in my life.

Imagine spending three hours a week in a dark and dreary classroom where the energy-saving teacher won't allow the lights to be turned on—a teacher with all the personality of a dial tone who drones on and on about a subject that is so painfully boring you pray for a sudden attack of the stomach flu as a way to escape.

Welcome to beginning bookkeeping.

I barely made it out of that class with a passing grade and then only because I actually showed up for every class. The whole thing was one big unintelligible blur. The teacher spoke a different language—one he forgot to teach to his students. I didn't know a debit from a credit on the first day of class or the last day, either.

What I did learn was that I could not understand anything about money and finance, and I had no plans to try to overcome this situation in the future.

Hindsight shows a much clearer picture. I know now that the problem wasn't my inability to learn. The problem was that from the first day of class I lost my confidence. As long as I believed

I could not learn this subject I was a lost cause. And every day of that long semester I reconfirmed my belief, right through the torturous final exam. From that day on I would avoid anything having to do with accounting, balance sheets, accounting records and the dreaded reconciliation. I lumped all money management under the dreadful heading of "bookkeeping."

I know now that the words I spoke to myself turned into my thoughts. Every thought was imposed on my subconscious and emerged as an attitude. That is when the words became powerful in my life. I had such an aversion to anything having to do with numbers. What I believed became a self-fulfilling prophecy. Without confidence that I could learn and understand how to manage money—both in deed and on paper—I was a exactly what I believed: A money idiot.

For much of my life after that disastrous bookkeeping class I lived under a dark cloud of worry that I would become financially destitute and homeless. I worried that eventually I'd find myself living under a bridge. As irrational as that might seem as you read it, according to a recent survey I'm not the only one of us who's ever had such a thought. Nearly 90 percent of women in this country admit they are financially insecure and worry about that bag lady thing, too.

Ladies, we need to talk. We don't have to accept financial insecurity as some kind of life sentence. And that constant and gnawing fear of becoming destitute? Forget it! We can do something about this.

We were created uniquely to birth children, to run households, to resolve problems, steer committees, host big events, and on and on it goes. Why do we struggle so when it comes to this matter of money? It's not for a lack of intelligence. The problem is we lack confidence. We're not sure where to start, who to ask or what to do.

Financial confidence is a choice. It's a matter of learning simple financial principles, then consciously applying them over and again until they become automatic responses—financial habits.

No matter how crazy you've been with money I'm pretty sure

I've got you beat. And I have it on very good authority that with God's power you can change. I hope that makes you excited about the future, makes you stop throwing away your bank statements, and gives you confidence that you can become the title of this book. At the very least, I hope you don't regret you bought it.

My journey into the credit-card abyss began quite innocently. I would never have considered my behavior irresponsible. I was simply agreeing to have it all now and pay for it later. I was pushing the envelope, living on the edge, going for the gusto because I would only go around once (obviously every marketing genius dreams of consumers like me). Throwing caution to the wind and living spontaneously were my definitions of enjoying life.

Me, irresponsible? No way! I was progressive, inventive, and creative. The challenge was that in order to carry off this persona I needed money—lots of it, and more than I happened to have at the time. I was driven to find new and better ways to mortgage my future; otherwise, I might be forced to stifle my marvelously whimsical tendencies and sudden inspirations.

I learned the hard way that irresponsible financial behavior eventually brings financial devastation. Activities meant to make me soar clipped my wings instead and sent me hurling into a pit of despair. My plan for freedom became my own prescription for bondage.

Financially irresponsible people are not bad people. They've developed bad habits—habits of omission, habits based upon what our gotta-get-it-all-right-now credit-crazed society insists is normal. They've chosen to get their financial "education" from the mega consumer credit industry that wants them to be in debt to the day they die. Because they've never been educated on matters of personal finance, they don't know when they're making mistakes; therefore, they don't learn from those mistakes until it's too late. The good news is bad habits can be unlearned and good habits learned. Having a desire to change is the key to becoming financially responsible.

If you are searching for quick fixes or ways to manipulate your present situation to qualify for more debt, this is not the book for you. However, if you're tired of always being broke, feel you cannot handle another monthly bill, are fresh out of juggling techniques, and fear things might never change, I'm glad we've found each other.

This is not a book about how to get more money. It's about how to become financially confident by learning how to manage what you already have. It's not a book equating poverty with spirituality. It is a book about right living, abundance, joy and the peace of mind that results from living a life that is pleasing to God.

And possibly most importantly, this is not an exhaustive treatment of the entire subject of personal finance and money management. That would not be a book—it would be a matching set of books and heavy ones at that.

I have taken the basic things you need to know and boiled them down, giving you the least you need to know to become financially confident.

In encouraging you to look deep into your personal belief system, I've had to come to a screeching halt on more than one occasion and search my own heart—that secret place deep within from which come my own attitudes and values. It continues to be a humbling experience, as I realize that only as I'm willing to be changed can I help others do the same.

I have so much to tell you, and I pray it will change your life the way it has mine. No matter where you are on the spectrum of financial responsibility, I have something wonderful to offer you—hope, confidence, and peace. God's peace.

Chapter 1

Confessions
of a Financially
Irresponsible Woman

"When money talks, it often says 'good-bye.'"
– Poor Richard Jr.'s Almanac (1906)

I had my first taste of freedom when I left home to attend college in California. I'll never forget my first week in Los Angeles. Like my first kiss, it was better than I'd ever imagined; and quite frankly, I wished it could last forever. The beautiful weather, the palm trees, the lights, and the excitement of the big city were far beyond anything I'd ever imagined during my numerous dreaming sessions. I just knew that college would be my paradise on Earth.

I intended to waste no time fulfilling my childhood promise: When I grew up I'd be rich. You see, I mistakenly equated my terminal sadness with the fact that I felt poor. It made perfect sense to me that being rich would produce happiness, and I just couldn't wait to be happy.

As California's newest Cinderella, I had been planning this transition from poor to rich for a long time. The moment I set foot on campus, my dream ceased being a fantasy and became a self-fulfilling prophecy.

I wasted no time opening a checking account. I knew I would need one to keep my money safe. I had a vague idea about how checking accounts worked. After all I did take high school book-keeping, painful as that experience was. And I must say that I was surprised that contrary to my preconceived notions, this device appeared to be simple and quite user-friendly. But I did- ·
n't know my checkbook carried a hidden danger.

The first time the idea crept into my mind I was with a group of friends—friends with cars and freeway savvy who introduced me to the world of California shopping malls. The idea of writing checks with no money in the account was about as insane an idea as I'd ever had. Even I knew that was not in keeping with acceptable accounting principles. I halfheartedly pushed the idea out of the way. And seconds later the idea returned.

The more I thought about it, the less outrageous it seemed. After all, who'd know? No one, not even the sales clerk, could know exactly how much money I had in my account. I could buy the things I wanted and, as a bonus, impress my friends with my fiscal prowess. Given sufficient time to get used to the con-cept—about thirty seconds—my idea didn't seem so insane after all; I'd do it just this once.

Unfortunately my crazy idea worked quite well. Not only were my friends impressed with my ability to keep up with them (they didn't come right out and say it, but I knew), the salesperson had to have been surprised by my ability to buy whatever I wanted. Acting rich gave me a sense of significance and, in turn, a fabulous feeling.

I figured out how to shop on Wednesday, get paid from my college library job on Friday, deposit the check on Monday and have time to spare to cover the checks I'd been writing all week long. Nobody was harmed because no one knew the difference.

It was exciting, too, because it felt like I was getting away with something—beating the system. Taking this kind of risk was exhilarating in some crazy way.

I didn't see what I was doing as wrong; I was simply being creative in my efforts to keep up the lifestyle to which I was becoming increasingly accustomed. Even when I bounced checks I didn't question the procedure I'd discovered. I was pretty easy on myself, concluding I wasn't exactly overdrawn, just under-deposited.

My checking account escapades were the start of a terrible destructive habit I allowed to take root in my life: I habitually engaged in the activity of acquiring first and figuring out how to pay later.

Somehow I made it through college without being subjected to public humiliation for having accounts closed due to excessive overdrafts. I escaped being arrested for kiting (the illegal practice of writing a bad check on one account to cover an overdraft on another).

I have no idea how much money I spent covering "insufficient funds" fees, but it had to have been a lot. Still, I refused to see my financial behavior as irresponsible or self-destructive. After all, like many college students, I'd just spent the better part of four years financially strapped. My creativity allowed me to spend what I didn't have at the moment to get what I couldn't live without. It was no big deal, and I didn't plan to do it forever.

When I married Harold shortly after graduation, I just assumed that I'd never have to worry about money again. After all, a man is supposed to take care of his wife, handle the finances, and make sure she, whose job it is to spend the money, has plenty of it. And this was no ordinary man. I married a banker.

In the absence of any counseling to the contrary, I figured that Harold would make loads of money and I'd create a lovely lifestyle for us. However in hindsight, the fact that I insisted we needed a credit card (just in case of emergency, of course) is clear evidence that deep inside I didn't feel he could handle his financial responsibilities and needed my intervention.

Plastic significance

The arrival of my first credit card triggered another insane idea in my head. I found that a gasoline credit card was far superior to spending the cash I might have in my wallet. It was easier to use plastic at the corner gasoline station. But the idea that went off in my head was far more dangerous than mere convenience. It shouted, "We get free gas whenever we want it!" Not having to worry about whether I had enough cash to pay for gasoline and choosing "full serve" to boot made me feel rich, dignified, and significant. Remember my contact with rich people had been limited, so the way they behaved was pretty much left up to my imagination. And I had one terrific imagination!

As a young girl I was blessed with a best friend, Judy. As a bonus to our friendship, Judy's parents were the richest people I'd ever known. They had a beautiful home and contemporary furnishings. Judy's dad had a telephone in his car, and her mom owned a successful business. Judy had what I understood to be unlimited access to her mother's accounts at all kinds of stores, not the least of which was the little corner grocery store.

Whenever I stayed over at Judy's—which was as often as I could finagle parental permission—I, too, became a rich kid. I was treated with the same privilege, love, and respect as a member of the Ellis family. I had acceptance and approval.

Judy and I had great freedom, which included unlimited entitlement to the little corner grocery store. We could buy anything we wanted anytime we felt like it. Anything. And we never needed money. The store owner, Rawley, made us feel like the most important girls in the world. Armed with Judy's signature alone, we could be on our way with the best selection of groceries any two teenagers could ever imagine. There were no limitations and no accountability—at least that was my perception.

I wonder now what kind of conversations resulted when Mrs. Ellis received that monthly bill. But for me that part of the story didn't exist. I'm sure I just assumed that because they were rich, eventual payment was just taken care of the same way a princess is taken care of. It just happens.

I lived for the weekends I would be able once again to experience firsthand the delights and freedom of being rich. To this day some of my fondest memories involve stayovers at Judy's house, where I received my first taste of significance and individual importance. It's no wonder I associated those wonderful feelings with money.

Fast forward to that gasoline card. As you might imagine, the initial excitement of that new gasoline entitlement wore off quickly when the monthly statement arrived. Surely someone had made a mistake. There's no way we'd filled up that many times. And the worst part? The gasoline company wanted full payment immediately. It was clear to me that we needed another brand of gasoline credit card to spread the purchases around. Then another and another.

Soon after, while I strolled through a local department store, a salesperson invited me to apply for the store's credit card. All I needed to qualify was a valid credit card, and my gasoline card would do. Talk about too good to be true! Of course I accepted with no regrets because once again I felt I was doing something noble—preparing for emergencies. Within just a few minutes I was entitled to lots more than just gasoline.

This revolving credit idea was really getting into my blood. It seemed so workable, so logical. A two hundred dollar purchase wasn't that at all. It was merely a ten-dollar monthly payment. Highly affordable in my book.

Of course intellectually I'm sure I knew better, but my ability to slip into denial transcended reason. I was able to remain comfortable because of my unique ability to justify and defend my activities.

My plastic safety net

It didn't take long for me to get caught up in the excitement of credit-card acquisitions. I was like a kid working on a baseball card collection. I never intended to really use them just to have these lines of credit all in place in case of emergencies. To me they were like seat belts, a first aid kit, jumper cables, and oat bran all rolled into one neat little package. I was convinced of my credit cards' ability to protect, nourish, comfort, and cure.

I had many "emergencies" over the following years and felt fully entitled to meet those needs using plastic. What I believed about them was absolutely true. They worked like a charm to relieve pain and worry. They offered asylum from the penalties of past-due property taxes and provided wonderful Christmas holidays for our two boys and extended families. Even the dentist and preschool accepted plastic. Credit cards worked perfectly in bridging the gap between what I'd determined was our woefully inadequate income and the cost of maintaining the minimum acceptable lifestyle—a lifestyle which demanded I provide for our two little boys, Jeremy and Josh, all the things I'd missed during my childhood.

Just when I thought it couldn't get any better, several of our credit cards offered that glorious added feature—the cash advance. Even though plastic was accepted nearly everywhere, there were occasions when I needed plain old green stuff, and the cash advance was right there to the rescue.

Because we kept up with the monthly payments and incurred a minimal number of late fees, we were fairly well qualified to land new forms of credit. I knew how the applications needed to read in order to be approved.

Because our credit report was pretty clean and Harold had an excellent job with a large California bank, credit wasn't the only thing we could acquire. We were able to purchase a home in a location where home values were escalating at an unprecedented rate. Our home in Orange County was increasing in value by at least 20 percent a year. At this rate our three-bedroom house would be worth $5 or even $10 million by the time we wanted to think about retirement. There was no need to start a savings program or plan for the future. When the time came, we'd put out a "For Sale" sign, sell the house quickly, gather up our millions, and sail off into retirement heaven. I had it all figured out.

Because I'd gotten into the habit of always spending more money than we had available, on quite a few occasions we had to refinance and take out second and even third mortgages on the house. After all, we had to eat. And with each new loan came another payment and greater necessity to find new sources of income. Of course, each time we refinanced I promised Harold that we'd pay off the debts and stop using credit as soon as we got things straightened out or after this thing or that thing happened.

But it never straightened out—for a million reasons, not the least of which was because we were young and figured we'd have plenty of time to save when our income increased. Unfortunately, as the years passed it was our financial obligations that increased.

Meltdown

After we'd been married for about twelve years, the minimum monthly payments on all our debts were totaling an amount dangerously close to our take-home pay. Most of our credit card credit lines were at the max, and juggling became a way of life. It was not unusual for us to use next month's check to cover this month's bills, or pay half the bills this month and half next. We were constantly chasing new forms of credit only to stay afloat.

I convinced my banker husband that his occupation would never cut it income-wise and that we should consider self-employment. It seemed like a good idea to me. Self-employed people, so I thought, were smart and wealthy. Self-employment would allow us to make the amount of money we needed. Harold wasn't all that enamored with the future the bank seemed to be offering and detested the politics he was being pressured to play. The banking industry was facing major revamping, and the idea of a new challenge and the bright hope of self-employment became attractive to both of us. We had dreams to fulfill and children to raise. We wanted a bright and inviting future, not one plagued with a constant shortage of money.

Once we opened our minds to such a drastic employment change, we became a couple of giant magnets to the many "opportunities" that existed. Harold had befriended a couple of his bank clients, and both of us couldn't help but be fascinated by their new German-made sports cars and very large, daily cash deposits. We were entertained in their Newport Beach homes, and their lifestyles really turned our heads. It didn't take long for their casual interest in us to become more deliberate. We were being sought after to join them in their mega-enterprise. They didn't pressure us. They simply befriended us and allowed us to view the good life. We checked the organization out as well as we could; however, our minds were already made up. I'm sure we were blind to warning signs that must have been screaming out to us.

We went to Atlanta as honored guests at the organization's annual sales meeting. Imagine how significant we felt as our friends who had made their way high into the organization introduced the banker who'd caught this marvelous organization's vision and was leaving sixteen years of tenure to become the newest company owner.

As thousands of people cheered, the entire episode was video-taped. I remember thinking how wonderful it was to have this momentous occasion recorded for our family's history and generations to come. I could see myself slipping behind the steering wheel of my own German-made sports car. I was so proud, so optimistic, and so happy for my husband who'd finally made a very difficult decision to leave his comfort zone and take an exciting risk.

Our trip back to California was energized by our resolve to be excellent employers and worthy stewards of this magnanimous new wealth that was about to be thrust upon us. Our plans were set and we wasted no time putting them into action.

Harold gave his resignation and customary notice to the bank, and we figured out how we would borrow the thousands of dollars we'd need to get into the business. A short-term loan was all we needed because this particular business was cash intensive. Repayment would be swift and sure.

Of course we needed a site for the business. (Did I mention it involved reselling poor quality merchandise? I mean very poor quality—so awful, in fact, this stuff would hardly have a chance of moving at a garage sale.) Since I'd dabbled in industrial real estate, I was able to pull off a lease and even earned a commission. Next we needed to furnish the place. We rented rooms full of office furnishings and accessories. One tenet of corporate headquarters was that each franchise needed to have a look of success to attract the caliber of people who would make sure that success continued.

We worked hard, but it was clear almost from the start that we'd been terribly misled about how easy it was going to be to get up and running profitably in a short time. Every cent we had borrowed plus every additional dollar we could rake off our credit-card limits was poured into the business. We felt we'd already put so much in we had to protect the initial investment. We justified letting our personal bills slide for a few months because we were still convinced the cash would start flowing. Then we'd get everything caught up and be none the worse for the temporary delay.

About two months into this self-employment nightmare I grew fearful. The honeymoon was over and the tension was setting in. We weren't able to hire all the people we needed in spite of very expensive advertising. Our furniture and warehouse rental payments were much larger than they seemed when we signed the paperwork. It was clear we were undercapitalized and overly optimistic.

And those two wonderful men who'd introduced us to our dream of a lifetime? They were gone and have remained gone to this day. Clearly their automobiles and homes were rented short-term to allow them to come into the area, fleece every sucker they could find, and leave before anyone could catch up with them. They were clever, too. We had nothing with which we could prove fraud or deception.

Four months from start to finish. The longest four months of our lives. We experienced every emotion of which we were capable, usually all at once.

As our hopes and dreams were being dashed, so was our relationship. Things hadn't been really terrific between us for quite a long time before this self-employment episode; but we passed that off as the financial strain we were under, my unwillingness to spend less, and insistence that he earn more. This new dream business had given us a common goal, and it temporarily rekindled our marriage.

It took four months for our dream to die. We buried it the day all the rented furniture was repossessed and we walked away from the building.

It was a painful and torturous death, and with it something in both of us died. Harold had gone from tenured bank employee to future millionaire to unemployed business owner in about sixteen weeks. To make matters worse, he had no unemployment benefits. Our income was zero, our home was moving closer to foreclosure each day, and we were defenseless against the pit of despair into which we were slipping. We had no idea what to do. When we needed each other the most, we were the least able to communicate or to even reach out to each other. We were two angry individuals completely isolated in our pain.

I cannot remember a time before or since that I have ever felt such utter defeat, pain, anger, and debilitating fear. When faced with life's challenges I had always had a plan B, another idea, an alternative. My controlling temperament had always pulled through, but I was completely unable to rescue this situation. We had bills on top of hills, debts to the ceiling, and, most seriously, we were in danger of losing our home.

And then God ...

It was September 1982. We'd just lost the business. I was paralyzed by fear and pain like I'd never known. I was fresh out of ideas. When I'd reached the end of myself and run out of schemes and solutions, God was able to get my attention.

It's not that I wasn't a Christian. I'd grown up in church, graduated from a Christian college, married a committed Christian, and was very active in church. The problem was I'd never allowed God to invade my life. I kept Him compartmentalized. My Christianity was convenient on Sundays or when missionaries visited. But when it came to my day-to-day life I had it figured out. I found security and dignity in the color and quantity of my credit cards and in my ability to borrow money. Now my house of cards was collapsing around me.

It was as if God turned on the floodlights of heaven, and for the first time I was able to acknowledge what I'd done. I saw what a horrible mess I'd made and what I'd done to my husband, my family, and myself.

Completely broken, I confessed that the manipulation, the scheming, deceit, and lying were sin. I begged for God's forgiveness (which of course was mine for the asking). I pleaded with God to let me keep my husband, my kids, and our home. I promised God on that day that I would do anything and everything necessary to pay back all the debt, to change my ways, and to find my security only in Him. Of course God forgave me the instant I sought forgiveness. All the debts were not mysteriously repaid or lost forever from the records of all the companies and individuals to whom we owed money. And my pain did not immediately disappear. But God forgave me.

I spent the next twelve years working hard and learning everything I could about myself. God marvelously provided a job for me—a real estate position where I was able to earn both a regular salary as well as commissions. We learned how to cut expenses and live without incurring new debt. There were occasions when we were slow learners, and we didn't do everything perfectly. But the point is this: As I was willing to change, God made those changes possible.

The ways that God provided and taught me are probably another book in themselves. But let me make this point absolutely clear: I allowed terrible habits to guide my life—actions I practiced habitually until they became almost automatic. Those habits when practiced over a long period of time had an accumulative, devastating effect.

Time to pay up

It took thirteen years, but we paid back the entire $100,000 in unsecured debts, plus all the interest and associated fees. We did not stiff one creditor for a single dime. We asked for no concessions and expected no discounts. I've come face to face with my compulsive overspending problem and am learning one day at a time how to deal with it and depend on God to meet our needs, instead of looking to credit as the solution.

As we've obeyed God's financial principles of giving, saving, and not spending more than we have, He's blessed us in ways you could never imagine. The irony is that now I have the wonderful privilege of helping people all over the country apply these same principles to their lives, get out of debt, and learn how to joyfully live beneath their means. It is possible to become responsible in areas where irresponsibility is the order of the day.

I'm still me

I have not had a personality transplant. I will always have compulsive tendencies. By God's grace, however, I'm learning how to control my compulsive nature, adopt good financial habits, and make up for lost time. After all, during the last twenty-five years, the years when we should have been preparing for the future by saving and investing, we were doing just the opposite. Considering the alternatives, we were thankful to return to point zero.

Wonderful things have happened since that day when I hit bottom. I've learned to allow God invade my life, not to just visit on Sundays. I've learned the necessity of obedience to God's Word and the joy and peace of mind that comes from a daily relationship with him.

Chapter 2

Where Is It Written "Women Don't Do Money"?

"Human beings, by changing the inner attitudes of their minds,
can change the outer aspects of their lives."
— William James, American philosopher

Lucy Ricardo taught me that being dumber than dirt is kind of cute. Her neighbor Ethel was a little smarter than Lucy but only occasionally managed to overcome Lucy's dumbness. And Gracie Allen (remember her?). Well, she was dumber than Lucy and Ethel put together.

Those girls could certainly spend the money, couldn't they? Thank goodness for Ricky, Fred, and George. Where would those women have been without the men to take care of them, protect them from themselves, and pay all the bills?

Those television husbands always managed to clean up their wives' messes. It didn't matter to what degree Lucy's own stupidity overwhelmed her; Ricky always had the solution and just in the nick of time. The women never had to think about money, and they never cared much about where it came from so long as it kept coming. I guess the men worked—that part of the plot was always a little foggy for me. Ricky left every morning for rehearsal; Fred hung out and collected rent. And George Burns? I haven't a clue what he did for a living. I don't think Gracie did either.

Those women didn't participate in the family finances, and that was the way we thought it was supposed to be. They spent their days poking into everyone's business and were hilariously consumed with how much trouble they could stir up.

The men were the protectors, the "bailer outers" and problem solvers. Of course, they handled all the finances. That was my favorite part. It was so romantic to be a bit helpless and silly. The secret was having a smart husband with unlimited sources of money who would always take care of everything.

Waiting for Prince Charming

As a little girl, I got the message that being protected and loved meant never having to know about money. I didn't get that message because I watched too much television—we didn't even have one. I learned it from real life.

In my world, women took care of the relationships and men took care of the money. Women were the emotional caretakers; men the wage earners.

I learned that men go to work, women shop and spend, and no one ever talks about it. My mother didn't handle any money. She had what she called "pin money," but it was not considered essential to her financial well-being or that of our family.

I learned that a good husband was measured by his ability to be a "good provider," which meant he earned the money, paid the bills, and made all the financial decisions.

I didn't learn appropriate and useful money skills because handling money was the exclusive territory of men. By default I learned that "women don't do money."

No wonder I breathed one big sigh of relief as I walked down the aisle. Not only was I marrying a terrific guy, I would no longer have to worry about "man stuff," like car trouble and money, because I'd found my provider, my caretaker, my man. I'd take care of the woman things and he'd do the man things. We never actually talked about it. Some things didn't require discussion.

I guess you know where this kind of flawed thinking got me. Let's put it this way: I didn't find marriage to be one lively episode of "I Love Lucy." My shenanigans with money weren't solved in thirty-minute segments. I didn't get a bail out and a fresh start every day as credits rolled by and the theme music played.

Distinctly different

I am not a feminist, "women's libber," or "N.O.W. gal." However, I do believe men and women are equal, and distinct creations. Praise God! I don't want to be like a man. I love being a woman. I have God-given characteristics as a woman that I acknowledge and embrace.

As women, we want happiness, we want significance, and we want to receive respect and honor from men.

We want to feel that we have a genuine purpose in life. We want to receive joy and satisfaction in our work, whether that work is in the home, outside the home, or both.

We want to feel secure, and we also want to feel valuable for our intelligence and management abilities.

I don't find any place in Scripture where women are relieved of the responsibility to be wise money managers. I don't know any verse that says men are to handle the money. Yet, there is a pervasive attitude, especially among Christians, that as head of the home, the man must make financial decisions and handle the money.

Personally, I believe some men use control of family finances as a way of keeping their wives dependent and subordinate.

Please don't misunderstand me. I can't think of a more noble calling than to be a wife and mother. I'm not suggesting for a moment that every woman must leave the home and join the working world. Nor am I suggesting that every woman must marry in order to be fulfilled and live a meaningful life. And I'm not saying that women should control the family purse. What I am saying is this: *Every woman, regardless of her marital status, age, strengths, or weaknesses, needs to know how to manage money confidently and effectively.*

God requires all people, men and women alike, to be good stewards, to work hard, to make wise decisions, to give back to Him, and to save for the future. I believe that the financial principles found in the Bible apply to both genders. Financial responsibility is for all of us.

God uses money to serve his purpose in our lives. He uses money to supply shelter, food, clothing—all of our needs and our wants, too. Money is the delivery system for the abundance we enjoy from the hand of a good and caring father. Every day is a test and a trust. God tests us with money to see how much he can trust us to be good caretakers of those resources.

Not her again!

I would love to meet the woman described in Proverbs 31. I didn't always feel so kindly toward her, however.

There was a time, I must admit, I dreaded Mother's Day—knowing that before I got out of the church service I'd surely find myself compared to the Proverbs 31 woman in some way or another.

Clearly, everything about her pointed out how miserably I was failing in the area of resource management. Rubbing her perfection in my face only made it worse.

As I've changed, I've changed my mind about her, too. She's become a role model to me—an example of a financially confident woman. I'm not sure I'll ever equal her amazing abilities, but she certainly sets an example worth emulating.

A truly good wife is the most precious treasure
a man can find!

Her husband depends on her,
and she never lets him down.

She is good to him every day of her life,
and with her own hands she gladly makes clothes.

She is like a sailing ship
that brings food from across the sea.

She gets up before daylight to prepare food
for her family and for her servants.

She knows how to buy land
and how to plant a vineyard,
and she always works hard.

She knows when to buy or sell,
and she stays busy until late at night.

She spins her own cloth,
and she helps the poor and the needy.

Her family has warm clothing,
and so she doesn't worry when it snows.

She does her own sewing,
and everything she wears is beautiful.

Her husband is a well-known and respected leader
in the city.

She makes clothes to sell to the shop owners.
She is strong and graceful,
as well as cheerful about the future.

Her words are sensible,
and her advice is thoughtful.

She takes good care of her family and is never lazy.
Her children praise her,
and with great pride her husband says,

"There are many good women, but you are the best!"

Charm can be deceiving and beauty fades away, but a
woman who honors the Lord deserves to be praised,

Show her respect—
praise her in public for what she has done.

Proverbs 31:10-31

A model worth emulating

Tell me, do you see a woman here who doesn't "do money"? Not a chance. She is resourceful, entrepreneurial, and a financial wizard. Did you notice how she buys land, plants a vineyard, and then knows when to sell? I'd love to walk down Wall Street with her. She's not sitting on the sidelines of the family financial decision-making because she thinks "women don't do money."

She doesn't mortgage her husband's future by getting into all kinds of debt that will keep them in bondage for many years to come. She doesn't think that it's her job to spend and his job to provide. And she's cheerful about the future. Let me tell you, if she had $100,000 in unsecured debt breathing down her neck with a drawer full of bills she's afraid her husband might find, cheerful would not be one of the ways her children described her.

Not only does she make her own clothes, she spins the yarn and weaves the cloth. And get this: She's developed her own line of beautiful fashions, which she sells to local boutiques. Her husband and kids are proud of her, which doesn't surprise me a bit.

This is one financially confident woman. There is absolutely no question in my mind that God honors this kind of pursuit and has given her profile to us as an example, a standard, an ideal.

A peek inside the mailbag

I get a lot of mail (and when I say a lot, I mean file drawers full of snail mail and email, too) from men and women, old and young, from every state in the U.S. and many foreign countries. These people are, for the most part, readers of *Debt-Proof Living*, a subscription newsletter I write and have published since 1992 (shameless plug).

Many of these letters start out: *"Dear Mary, What I'm about to tell you I've never told another soul...."* I'd estimate that about 85 percent of the letters I receive are from women, and of that number at least 50 percent are from women in pain who tell me of their frustration and struggles with money. I've learned so much about myself and others through this unique form of education. Take a peek into my letter files:

"I'm so discouraged. No matter how hard I try, there's never enough money. I just don't know what to do."

"I've tried to save, but every time I put some money away, something comes up. Right now I have $1,100 in bills I can't pay. The creditors are calling and I'm terrified."

"I'm a housewife with three girls. We live paycheck to paycheck. My husband refuses to admit just how bad things really are. I have no idea where his paycheck goes. If only I knew someone to lend us some money."

"I feel as if I am sinking in an abyss of financial ignorance."

"My heart is so heavy. . . . I hate myself when I fail over and over. I was doing so good at not using plastic but have fallen off the wagon again. We are at least $1,000 short every month and I am dying inside."

"We're always in some crisis about money, but my husband just ignores it. I just don't know where the money goes."

"He is a good provider most of the time, but during the slow months it's really terrible. I worry so much about money I'm making myself sick."

"I've always wanted to buy a home, but I think that will never happen. My husband left me with the kids and all the bills."

"When he died, I was shocked to find out the condition of our finances. For forty-eight years I had no idea what was going on because he always handled the money."

"I'm so sick of always being broke and having to pretend that everything is okay."

"If I have it, I spend it. It's like I can't help myself. For me going shopping is like playing roulette, I just never know what's going to happen."

"Money is just too hard for me. I feel like a failure."

"I only wish I had the ability to earn more money. Things are very tough and I just don't know how we'll make it."

"I hope you can help me. I'm all alone for the first time in twenty-eight years. I don't even know where to start."

"I thought the insurance money would be plenty. I realize now that I should have looked for someone to tell me how to invest it. Between lending it to the kids and fixing up the house, it's just about gone and I have no idea what I'll do when it is."

These women have reached a critical point. They need the skills and the knowledge to competently manage money, but they don't know what to do to take control. Their situations are controlling them, and that is a terrible place to be.

Maybe you, too, have felt some of the same painful, frustrating, discouraging, hopeless, and scary feelings like those you've just read.

Perhaps you've secretly wondered, what's the matter with me? I can't control my spending, and I feel anxious and frustrated about money. I have no one to take care of me, and I don't know what I'm doing. I'm afraid something terrible is going to happen—and on and on.

Fiscal reality

A woman who has never been exposed to the subject of money management is typically afraid of making financial decisions. She doesn't feel capable, and doesn't feel she can trust herself to make these kinds of changes. She'd just as soon someone else make all the financial decisions for her. I say this because I know that was true for me. *Don't make me think! Just tell me what to do.* Have you ever thought those words—or said them out loud?

You might believe that money is not an important concern because you have a husband to make it, handle it, and manage it. Perhaps you are a young woman still living at home, waiting for Prince Charming to show up on his white horse with a promise that you will never have to worry your pretty little head about a thing.

Listen: You have to look beyond today. Chances are great that sometime during your lifetime things will change. You will be required to skillfully manage money, and you might not have a great deal of warning.

There's also the distinct probability that if you are married, your husband would love for you to start participating as a partner in the money area of your lives. For those of you who have children, consider what a terrific parenting team you and your husband make. The same could happen in your financial life.

Greater numbers of women are becoming money conscious because women are managing more money than ever before.

More women are reaching top positions in the workplace. We are enjoying better female earning capacity and a highly educated female population.

In fact, women are expected to control 60 percent of the wealth in the U.S. by 2010. Yet despite all they have achieved, women in this country still feel financially insecure. Want to know just how insecure?

Ninety percent of women who participated in a 2006 survey commissioned by Allianz Insurance said they feel very insecure about money. Eighty percent of these self-professed financially ignorant women worry about ending up destitute—they fear becoming bag ladies. And this even applied to those women who earned more than $100,000 annually.

Many (80 percent to be exact) of those surveyed say they will depend on Social Security to be their source of income during their golden years. Over half of women surveyed have more than $5,000 in household debt and nearly 30 percent said they have over $20,000.

Seventy-two percent of women say retirement is their primary investment goal; yet nearly half (48 percent) do not participate in a retirement savings plan and 60 percent have not taken the necessary steps to prepare for retirement.

Here's another shocker: Women save only half of what men do, on average.

Additionally, according to the United States Bureau of the Census the following is true:

- ❖ Forty-eight percent of women aged sixty-five and older are or will be widowed.

- ❖ Fifty percent of women who married within the last twenty years will divorce.

- ❖ Ten percent will remain single.

The message is quite sobering, isn't it? You have a nine out of ten chance that at some point in your life, you will be solely responsible for your own financial situation. Will you know what to do?

Whether you are currently using them or not, you need to keep up your skills and your education so that in the event of a major life change you will have the confidence necessary to deal with it.

While it is slowly closing, the wage gap still exists in this country. Women earn seventy-seven cents for every dollar earned by men. That alone is a good argument for why women, above all, need to possess excellent financial planning and management skills.

Whether presently you are solely responsible for your financial well-being, you share it with your partner, or you want to be prepared for any eventuality—there's no time like the present to start learning how to become a financially confident woman.

A wife who says, "My husband handles that sort of thing," is likely giving away a huge part of her life.

The traditional relationship where the wife is not involved with the family finances (being given a couple of hundred bucks a week for groceries and household expenses doesn't count as being involved in the family finances) is not only shortsighted, it is just plain stupid. The other extreme, where the husband opts out of all financial matters, leaving all the bills and financial planning to his modern wife, is no better.

Typically one of the two partners in a marriage is more naturally gifted with numbers. Terrific! Then that person should keep the records but not make all the decisions.

Becoming more knowledgeable about money means more than just paying the bills or balancing the checkbook. It means understanding money—compounding interest, credit, debt, and how to keep more of it.

In my home I am the one who's not good with numbers, so Harold balances the checkbook. It's not that I don't know how or couldn't do it if he wasn't available. And he's terrible in the kitchen, so I do the cooking. It has nothing to do with gender, but talent. When it comes to major financial decisions and the monthly bills, we review everything together and the decision making is a joint effort.

The nurturing female

Men and women bring different things to a marriage. Being a woman, I know that I have God-given strengths by virtue of my female genes. I'm a nurturer. I'm more sensitive to detail and able to keep track of where things are and where they're supposed to be. I love to watch things grow. Knowing everyone is safe and tucked in at night somehow gives me a feeling of well-being and security.

Those are characteristics God placed inside of me, and guess what? Those parts of my personality make me the best one to look after our investments. They need to be nurtured, allowed to grow in the safest place possible so they are all cozy and warm.

Harold and I are a team; and since we've learned to be team players in this area of personal finance, our relationship has grown tremendously, as has our financial picture.

Stop for a moment and think about how smart, clever, capable, and responsible you are in so many areas of your life.

Perhaps you single-handedly run a household, possess excellent skills as scheduler, cleaner, chauffeur, chef, dietitian, nutritionist, tutor, athletic coordinator, laundress, seamstress, landscape artist, florist, purchasing agent, and nurse.

Perhaps you are very successful in your career and have gained the respect of your peers in the professional world. There is absolutely no reason you cannot add competent money manager and financial planner to your list of abilities and skills.

Money management needs to become as important in your life as all the other skills you've learned. A financially confident woman is a woman who has the knowledge, ability, and desire to behave in a financially responsible manner. The designation is available to anyone.

Chapter 3

Responsible Is Not Another Word for Dull and Boring

"When we were children, we thought and reasoned as children do.
But when we grew up, we quit our childish ways."
— 1 Corinthians 13:11

At first glance the ad for a part-time college library assistant seemed like the perfect job for me. Since I was transportationally challenged, working on campus would have its advantages.

My interview was not as idyllic, however. Miss Agnes Holt could have been cast as the stereotypically stern, joyless librarian. She had the part down pat. She also had great intuition. Prior to hiring me as her assistant she gave me quite a little lecture on responsibility.

It didn't take long for me to develop a healthy fear of the woman and an equally healthy determination that I wouldn't let her consecration to responsibility rub off on me. Like a uniform, I slipped into my responsible self during work hours and shed it as quickly as possible when my time was up.

Why is it that the whole idea of being responsible sounded so matronly, so boring, so downright dull? To me, responsible was what divided the dull personalities from those who had a life.

In my world, responsible was what kept the less-than-fun group hopelessly dormitory-bound. The risk takers were anything but responsible. I guess you might say irresponsible was where the action was. It didn't take me long to decide where I wanted to align myself. I looked at it this way: Responsibility tied people down, so irresponsibility should free them up. Thus, my experiences with throwing caution to the wind and living for the moment began.

With that background I find it quite amazing that this is a book about responsible living. God's willingness to redeem even the most unlikely people is something that continues to amaze me. Make no mistake, however; this is not a book on how to become matronly, boring, and dull. This is a book about financial responsibility. It is not a book about budgets. If you ask me, there are already too many books on budgets.

This is a book about the miracles that can happen when irresponsible financial habits are forever replaced with responsible ones.

Since my younger days, I have learned that it is possible to be responsible and fun-loving. It is possible to be financially mature and contemporary. It is possible to be responsible and spontaneous. Responsibility simply means being accountable, and that is a good thing.

No matter what the terms *responsible* and *irresponsible* mean to you, I hope that for the next couple hundred pages you'll be able to set aside any preconceived notions, sit back, and enjoy. Maybe you'll learn something new. Then again, you might discover you're one of those to-be-envied sorts for whom financial responsibility comes naturally—and you're a fun person, too. If so, your habits are what the rest of us wish to emulate. We want to be like you.

The basic plan

My goal is that by the time you finish this book you will have the basic tools to:

❖ assess your relationship with money,

❖ take control of irresponsible behaviors,

❖ replace them with behaviors that are responsible, and

❖ see that those positive financial behaviors become lifelong habits.

First, we're going to take a quick look at how our beliefs, attitudes, and values determine how we behave with money.

Next, we will tackle the whole idea of how repeated behaviors become habits whether they're positive behaviors or not. We will see how we can choose to change our behavior by going back to examine our beliefs that are responsible for our inappropriate behavior. It's like finding the offending "bug" and fixing the system.

We will then identify the habits of financially responsible women and set out to purposely do the things they do; we will replace our bad habits with actions that are in accordance with God's word.

The Am-I-Financially Irresponsible? Self-Diagnosis Test

Directions: Answer yes or no to the following statements.

1. I have nothing close to a reasonable knowledge of my income, fixed expenses, irregular expenses, and net worth.

2. I don't have the discipline to be good with money.

3. I am near, at, or over the limit on my credit cards.

4. I've bounced more than three checks in the past year.

5. I often use this month's income to cover last month's bills.

6. I can't imagine living without credit.

7. I've never been concerned about money because I have a spouse who takes care of it.

8. I worry about money quite a bit.

9. I hide the mail.

10. I don't have a formal savings program.

11. If I had more money I'd be just fine.

12. I have lied to my spouse or creditors about making payments.

13. I know I should give back to God but I just don't have enough money right now.

14. I've taken a cash advance on one credit card to make the payment on another card.

Scoring: If you answered no to every question, you are my heroine. You are a financially responsible person.

If you answered "yes" to one or two questions, your tendencies lean toward responsible, but you should consider these areas to be red flags.

Three to five "yes" answers are a definite sign that you're headed down the road to financial trouble. I pray you will see the need to turn around immediately.

"Yes" on six or more? There's no doubt about it—we need each other. I recommend you not leave home until you finish this book.

MONEY DO'S AND DON'TS FOR WOMEN

Do	Don't
Be a giver.	Be a taker.
Save a portion of every paycheck and other money at the time it flows into your life.	Wait to see what's left at the end of the month.
See yourself as an equal contributor to the welfare and well-being of your family.	Consider yourself a second-class partner if you don't happen to earn a separate paycheck.
Nurture your financial identity.	Depend on your partner or another person to make your financial decisions.
Develop and maintain skills so that you are capable of earning a living.	Let your education go to waste by allowing your job skills to become obsolete.
Communicate openly about all areas of personal financial planning.	Assume anything.
Plan ahead for emergencies.	Fool yourself by thinking challenges of a financial nature will never come upon you and your family.
Take pride in your position as manager or co-manager of the most important organization on earth—your family.	Ever put yourself down.
Consider debt something to be avoided if at all possible. It really is a four-letter word.	Count your credit limits as part of your income or as an entitlement to have what you cannot afford with your regular income.
Order copies of your credit reports at least annually.	Assume the credit reporting agencies never make a mistake.

Chapter 4

Time Out for a
Values Inventory

*"You created me and put me together. Make me wise
enough to learn what you have commanded."*
– Psalm 119:73

What are your money beliefs? Do you even have a clue? Could you articulate them if it were really important to do so? Could you write them down?

It's possible you've never even thought about your money beliefs beyond knowing that you like money and never seem to have enough. How you deal with money—your money behavior— is determined by what you think about money—your money beliefs. Your money behavior is an outward display of what you believe about money and its role in your life. If you've never thought about this before, it's likely that those beliefs are nebulous and buried somewhere in your subconscious mind.

Behaviors

Behaviors are symptoms of our internal beliefs. Trying to

manage symptoms while ignoring the underlying cause is a waste of time and energy. Haven't we learned that from all the diets and budgets we've tried? Sure, they might work for a day or a week, maybe longer, but in time diets and budgets fail because they just don't get down into the root of the problem.

Beliefs

A belief is a feeling of certainty about what something means. It is a statement we make about ourselves or the world. Clearly, it is possible to have personal beliefs that are not based in truth. Dangerous perhaps, but indeed possible. Once a false belief is identified, it is possible to dump it and replace it with one that is true.

Attitudes

A group of beliefs regarding the same object or subject produces an attitude. Once an attitude is formed, behavior regarding that object becomes pretty much automatic.

If my attitude toward dogs is one of fear, it's quite likely I had a bad experience with a dog somewhere along the line. So every time I encounter a dog, I experience fear—an automatic response based on a group of beliefs. Each of us has a belief system that is made up of many beliefs that in turn produce many attitudes.

Values

Values are specific types of beliefs that are so important and central to one's belief system they act as life guides. Values are central to a person's personality and are responsible for motivations and important decisions that have far-reaching implications.

Typically a person will have hundreds of thousands of beliefs, a thousand or so attitudes, and around a dozen values. When it comes to money, many of us live under false beliefs that greatly affect our lives.

Money training

Your money beliefs are a mirror that reflects the money attitude and beliefs of one or both of your parents and those of the segment of society in which you live. All of these have taught you a lot about how you as a woman should behave with money—what you should and should not do, and what you can and cannot do.

Generally speaking, all money beliefsare a variation on one of two themes: Money is evil; money is good. Whether we worship money or hate it, when we hold it responsible for our happiness we give it power. Whether consciously or subconsciously, we choose the role money plays in our lives. So we—not our money or lack of it—are solely responsible for our attitudes, beliefs, actions, and happiness.

As a little girl, you were like a sponge. You soaked up beliefs. You watched and listened. Maybe you absorbed fear, perhaps adoration. You may have formed beliefs about being undeserving or incompetent. What you learned, starting with your first moment on earth, has contributed to your adult attitudes and beliefs about how to get what you want and need. All of these beliefs have determined what you feel you deserve—if you think you are smart enough to manage money, or if you believe you must forever depend on someone else to get what you need.

The beliefs and therefore the attitudes you have about money have a lot to do with why you always spend more money than you have, why you don't believe you will ever get ahead, why you feel so controlled by your finances, why you can't get enough money, or why you don't believe you deserve anything.

I received a letter from a woman who told me of her struggle with letting go of false money beliefs. As the oldest child of missionaries, she spent her early childhood and teenage years in a foreign country.

Somehow during those years she developed a false belief that to serve God in a meaningful way you must live in poverty. After all, why else would her family be so poor while the carnal Christians "back home" in secular occupations lived in luxury? Her parents would often tell her that while they had little money and material possessions they were rich because they were serving the Lord.

Years passed and this woman became a mother and wife. She became one of those "carnal Christians." She felt guilty for having nice things, for making more money in a month than her family had for an entire year on the mission field. Once she was able to dig through all her emotions and get to the heart of the matter, she discovered her false beliefs regarding money were keeping her from enjoying all the blessings God had given to her.

Once you accept the fact that perhaps some of the things you believe about money might be defective or downright false, you can begin the process of changing your money beliefs, and thus your money behaviors. You will be able to let go of old beliefs that keep you stuck in either hating or worshiping money.

If you have been irresponsible or reckless with money, have allowed credit to control your life, have gotten into a tiny financial mess or one of behemoth proportions, or have failed to participate in the financial aspects of your home, it is not because there's something wrong with you. You are not fiscally defective! It's just that somewhere along the way you've picked up false beliefs about money and the role it plays in your life.

Taking responsibility

We are responsible for our own beliefs, feelings, and attitudes. We have to look to ourselves when it comes to doing something about our problems with money or lack of understanding about it. Blaming money, or the lack of it, for our problems and behaviors is no different than blaming others or God for our misery. We choose the role money plays in our lives, and taking responsibility for that is the first step in making necessary changes. The first step in taking responsibility for our beliefs is finding out what they are.

Are you ready to examine your current beliefs and attitudes about money? Perhaps you're unsure what yours are. Frankly, I'd be a little surprised if you weren't.

Following are common beliefs and attitudes about money. Perhaps you'll find some of each of the attitudes in your own life, perhaps none. Regardless, learning about others' beliefs may help you figure out what your own attitudes are. Once you know what they are, you'll be able to examine them, identify those that are based in truth, and let go of false, destructive beliefs and attitudes.

Destructive and Self-Defeating Money Attitudes

Money as an object of worship

If someone had accused me of worshiping money, I would have said, "No way. I'm a Christian and that's the last thing a Christian would ever do!" I've since learned that is also a false belief because many people worship money, Christians and nonbelievers alike.

Worship is the adoration, homage, or veneration given to a deity. It's that deep and reverent kind of love we're supposed to reserve for God. Changing the focus from God to money is a rather foolish thing to consider.

The act of worship, something our souls long for, requires these three elements:

1. A worshiper

2. Something to worship

3. The worshiper's willingness to be controlled by the thing or person worshiped.

If I choose money to be the thing I worship, for example, I voluntarily place myself under the control of money. I give up control and allow money to have authority over my life. I become subservient to it.

Sounds pretty sick when we put it into words, doesn't it? The person who worships money is convinced that money, and enough of it, holds the key to a perfect life. She might also believe it is responsible for love, freedom, success, and joy.

I spent years of my life worshiping money. Getting more and more of it became my central focus.

I was in awe of what it was supposed to do in my life; because my ego was insatiable, more money was never enough.

I guaranteed myself a life of unhappiness because I was always waiting to be happy until I had enough money. I was obsessed with money. No wonder I was so miserable.

God's word has a lot to say about money. In fact, while I haven't actually counted, I am told there are more verses in the Bible about money than any other subject, second only to love. Clearly, money is important to God.

"The love of money causes all kinds of trouble. Some people want money so much that they have given up their faith and caused themselves a lot of pain." 1 Timothy 6:10.

"Don't fall in love with money. Be satisfied with what you have. The Lord has promised that he will not leave us or desert us." Hebrews 13:5.

The message is clear: We must not worship anything or anyone other than God himself. Nothing and no one other than God should be allowed to sit on the throne of our lives. It is impossible to worship both God and money (see Luke 16:13). There's only room for one on that throne.

God says that we are not to worship any god except Him, that he is a jealous God who wants us to love and obey His laws (see Exodus 20:2-6).

God's rules make a lot of sense. They aren't harsh or inconsiderate of our needs, and by following them the quality of our lives can be greatly improved.

When we don't honor God and we divert our worship to anything or anyone else, misery results. Take it from me, it is easy to allow money to become a god.

Money as a mood changer

Money can be as powerful a mood changer as the most potent tranquilizer—and as habit forming. Spending money, whether we have it or not, has become a socially acceptable practice—especially if we can justify the act because we've had a terrible week and deserve to buy a little something nice for ourselves.

When it comes to needing to snap out of it or get over it, spending money often does the trick. Yet it is a poor tranquilizer because the satisfaction of the purchase wears off quickly. It takes a bigger fix the next time to achieve the same level of mood change.

I spoke with a friend one day who through tears described how she is compelled to buy something for herself every day. If she doesn't, she feels so bad she can't stand it. Buying something somehow provides an anesthetic effect for her bad feelings and gives her something to look forward to. She has been completely unable to give up this shopping ritual, even though she has become buried in secret debt and has closets full of new merchandise for which she has absolutely no use.

There's real danger in using money to alter our moods because it is very easy to become addicted to the act. We are easily addicted beings. Some people medicate strong feelings with a drug of choice, others with a compulsive behavior. For many women, shopping is an effective way to deal with fears and feelings of insignificance and loneliness. They buy something pretty in the same way a mother hands over a pacifier to a fussy baby.

Money measures success

Do you relate poverty with evil and prosperity with good? Align poverty with stupidity and prosperity with intelligence? That's what all our childhood fairy tales taught, didn't they?

No wonder those who believe that wealth and success go hand in hand feel personal failure whenever they experience a lack of money. On the other hand, if they have a streak of "good luck," women who share this particular attitude about money then feel they have value because of this "success." If you believe that your value depends on how much money you have, your status and self-image fluctuates along with your bank balance.

This false money belief can be very tempting because of the emphasis society places on the partnership of success and money. It's a rare person who does not immediately define success by using the word money.

What is success anyway? Is it reached when one makes $200,000 a year or when a child's life is changed for eternity through the faithfulness of a Sunday School teacher? Is it winning an Academy Award or writing lyrics to a song that will touch the hearts of people for centuries to come? I don't know all the answers; but it seems to me that when we get really honest, true success is often far removed from dollar signs.

It is a freeing thing to separate the issue of money from your life's work. Once money is a non issue, you will be free to concentrate on what really matters and what will last long after you're gone.

Money buys love and approval

Do you feel driven to go on a spending spree, justifying it as benevolence? Do you tell yourself, "It's for the grandchildren," or "I'm buying for others"?

Are you buying gifts or are you attempting to buy approval and love? Are you being generous or purchasing obligation?

Why is it that you always have to take the largest gift to the party or crave the feeling of status you get when you pick up the tab at the restaurant?

The person who is driven to use money to gain affection, approval, and love doesn't feel she deserves approval and love for being just who she is. She is driven to sweeten the pot with money and things.

Parents with this false money belief often overindulge their children with everything under the sun. They have the underlying goal of earning their children's love and approval.

Money is evil; poverty is righteous

There is a money belief that goes like this: Money is evil, and those who have it are greedy, dishonest, sinister, and generally corrupt. If you have this belief, to be good you must be poor. Poverty is equated with goodness. There is an underlying fear that opening one's life to money is a clear invitation for evil to come in and take over. Hate and fear of money become the unspoken rationale for losing, mishandling, and being unable to handle money. I've known people who even refuse to accept it. They seem to possess an internal terror of losing their goodness to money.

There are women who have become addicted to poverty and have a very difficult time giving up the false belief that money is evil, as are those who have it.

Those who hold this money belief equate their poverty with martyrdom and a high level of virtue. The woman with this belief feels more righteous than the "money-grubbing" individuals around her who are obsessed with materialism. Because of this belief, she is likely a compulsive underearner, hesitant to accept payment for work she does. Her volunteerism is usually excessive, and she feels that her eternal rewards negate the necessity of fair payment here on earth. What money she does have or manages she hoards, compulsively stashing and investing and then "righteously" living on a ridiculously low, poverty-level income.

Perhaps you grew up in a family with very low financial means. Your parents, in dealing with the situation, taught you the foolishness of money and the vanity that accompanies it—telling you that there are more important things in life than money. Money was a vice. Of course these things are true in some ways, but the message you received was that if you are to be a woman of virtue you need to avoid money lest it be allowed to corrupt your life.

Perhaps you didn't learn that money is the result of a job well-done and that money can be used in a remarkable way to demonstrate your commitment to God's principles.

Money is limited

Another destructive belief goes something like this: The money I have is all I'll ever have; when it's gone, that's all there is.

As a kid I remember feeling this way about colognes and other precious commodities. Because I feared that when these products were gone there would be no more, I never used them. I only looked at them. I still wonder whatever happened to those little navy blue bottles of Evening in Paris.

This belief causes paralyzing fear of inflation, interest rates, cost of living, and the future. The most terrible thing about this belief is that it's self-fulfilling. Because we fear there will be no more money, we make sure that's exactly what happens. It's a lot like thinking, "I just know I can't do it"—and sure enough, you can't.

Women who believe money is scarce are often debilitated by the possibility of making mistakes. Because there's no room for error, there's no ability to take risks.

Healthy Money Beliefs and Attitudes

You might be amazed to know that the Bible has over two thousand references to the subject of money. It's a money reference guide. God's Word, the source of all truth, is the place to find guidance for establishing our beliefs and attitudes.

Money is a tool

Money is a handy convenience. Without it we'd have to carry around chickens and pigs to trade for goods and services that we need.

We exchange money for our skills and abilities, so, in a way, it is a tangible representation of our life's energy. Money is a tool that God gives to us—all of us, men and women alike—because He is the giver of skills and abilities.

Money is powerless

Money has no power of its own, in the same way your sewing machine or electric mixer have no inherent ability. (I'd be very interested in a lawn mower or vacuum cleaner that had the ability to self-operate, wouldn't you?)

The truth is that no matter how fancy, how turbocharged, how modern or technically capable, any tool left in the closet or used contrary to the purpose for which it was intended is not going to produce the best results; and in some cases, the results can be negative.

The best example of this is the woman who intended to wax her car and picked up the power sander instead of the power buffer. They looked alike. Enough said.

Money is a neutral commodity

It's what we do with a tool that counts. The way we manage money is a direct reflection of our commitment to obey God and serve others. God honors right attitudes, and when a godly belief system and a set of life values are reflected through our finances, God is glorified. He blesses those whom He can trust.

We are not to worry about from where money will come. Employers (or pensions, bonuses, real estate income, support, unemployment checks, or any other entity) are not the source of our income. They are simply the conduits through which God delivers it.

God is the source because He is the one who has given us the skills and abilities to work. Jobs may come and go, stock markets may crash, real estate values may fall off the face of the earth, but the Source is the same yesterday, today, and forever. Our job is to be faithful, diligent, and trustworthy stewards.

Listen to the words of Jesus:

> *"So I tell you, don't worry about everyday life ? whether you have enough food, drink, and clothes. Doesn't life consist of more than food and clothing? Look at the birds.*

They don't need to plant or harvest or put food in barns because your heavenly Father feeds them. And you are far more valuable to him than they are.

"Can all your worries add a single moment to your life? Of course not. And why worry about your clothes? Look at the lilies and how they grow. They don't work or make their clothing, yet Solomon in all his glory was not dressed as beautifully as they are. And if God cares so wonderfully for flowers that are here today and gone tomorrow, won't he more surely care for you? You have so little faith!

"So don't worry about having enough food or drink or clothing. Why be like the pagans who are so deeply concerned about these things? Your heavenly Father already knows all your needs, and he will give you all you need from day to day if you live for him and make the Kingdom of God your primary concern. – Matthew 6:25-33

Here are five simple money rules that when followed will solve all of your financial problems:

1. Give some away.

2. Keep some.

3. It is better not to borrow; but if you cannot avoid it, repay the debt quickly.

4. Do not spend money that doesn't belong to you yet.

5. Do not fall in love with money.

Money is to be a nonemotional subject. We are not to love money or hate it, be fearful of not having enough or worried about having too much.

We are to be comfortable with money, not anxious about it or careless with it. We are not to hoard it, nor are we to throw it away. That kind of financial balance is called solvency. Solvency occurs when money takes its proper place in our lives as a tool with which to serve the Lord, not as a filler of empty souls.

Happiness and contentment

Each of us has a body, an ego, and a soul. Our egos are in search of happiness; our souls long for contentment.

Your ego is not a bad thing. It's that part of you that includes your personality—your thinking, feeling, and acting self. Your ego is responsible for your style and personal tastes. Your ego produces emotions and desires—and I mean all kinds of desires, from little, so-so ones to those that scream out to be satisfied. Some desires are for needs, others for wants.

Face it. Satisfying a desire produces happiness, and it usually takes money to fulfill desires. Anyone who says money can't buy happiness has never bought new carpeting or a new car, or seen the look on a child's face on Christmas morning. The frustrating thing is that this kind of happiness is temporary. It always wears off.

Think back to a time when you longed for something. I mean really longed and yearned. You were nearly obsessed by your desire and could think of little else. Maybe it was your first car or a certain article of clothing or a new piece of furniture. When you finally got it you were happy beyond belief. But the happiness wore off, didn't it? That's because desires once satisfied do not stay satisfied. Gratification received from fulfilled desires is, at best, temporary. That's how our minds and emotions work.

Your soul, your spiritual nature seeks contentment—satisfaction with what you have, whatever your situation might be. Contentment is a learned behavior, an acquired skill. It doesn't just happen when you fall into the right set of circumstances. Contentment cannot be purchased, and that's the best news because it means contentment is available to everyone, no matter what their financial situation might be.

I believe that this longing for contentment within every person was placed there by God Himself. Further, I also believe He made that desire so unique that only a personal relationship with Him through His Son, Jesus Christ, can bring lasting satisfaction and the contentment our souls long for.

Once you understand that fulfilling the desires of ego produces temporary satisfaction and fulfilling the desires of your spirit brings lasting satisfaction, you can stop hoping to find lasting contentment in a new sofa, or joy and peace in new carpeting. Sure, your new sofa and carpeting will likely bring you happiness for some period of time. And that's wonderful. But you will quit looking to material things to produce the contentment your spirit seeks. You will instinctively know the difference between momentary pleasure and deep-seated contentment. What a change that will make in your life. Contentment has a way of quieting insatiable desires. Contentment is the best antidote for an overly needy ego.

How to Change Your Money Behaviors

I discovered a secret, and I'm going to share it with you. If you want to change your money behavior, don't start with the behavior itself. I know that's what you've always tried to do in the past. Like another diet or another budget, however, attempting to manipulate the symptoms without taking notice of the belief behind the behavior will only result in failure. The behavior might change temporarily, but not permanently.

You must trace the behavior back to the beliefs that are responsible for that action.

One of the best ways to get in touch with feelings and beliefs is to write. I think you'll find journaling to be very helpful in identifying your money beliefs. The written word has a wonderful way of giving substance and form to nebulous thoughts. You can identify which, if any, of your beliefs are false; and you can write about the healthy beliefs, attitudes, and values you want to bring into your life.

With time and commitment to this project you will have developed powerful information and insight and you'll be ready to form new and healthy lifelong habits.

One word of caution: The more central a belief, the more resistant it is to change; and the more impact such change will have on the overall belief system. If one of your central beliefs changes, expect rather profound changes in how you think about many things.

Learning to view ourselves as deserving of every good and perfect gift from our heavenly Father doesn't mean indulging in every selfish desire we might have.

Living abundantly means resting in the calm assurance that God, the Creator of the universe, loves you and me. He owns everything there is and knows our needs and the desires of our hearts.

Living abundantly frees us to neither hate nor love money. Only when money is not the central focus of our lives can we stand back and see it as it truly is, and let it take its rightful place in our lives.

"I will bless you with a future filled with hope—
a future of success, not of suffering."
– Jeremiah 29:11

Chapter 5

Re-forming Your Habits

"We are what we repeatedly do. Excellence, then,
is not an act, but a habit."
– Aristotle

H ave you ever noticed how bad habits seem to come from nowhere, sneak in when you're not paying attention, and make themselves right at home? Mine remind me of weeds that push their way into a beautiful garden and arrogantly use their strength and amazing resistance to gain the upper hand. My good habits, on the other hand, are more like delicate sweet peas that require coaxing, cultivation, nurturing, and undaunted encouragement to build strong roots and grow into something of beauty. If only my good habits were as prolific as my bad ones.

Habits are those consistent, almost unconscious responses and behaviors that determine our effectiveness or ineffectiveness. A habit is a powerful force with the unique ability to be a best friend or a worst enemy. Our habits—how we behave day to day—are the outward and constant expressions of our character. What we do habitually reflects who we are.

Some of us act as though our habits were issued at birth and, good or bad, are as predetermined as our blood type and about as likely to ever change. Nothing could be further from the truth. It is possible to learn good habits and unlearn bad ones, no matter how ingrained or deep seated they may be.

Habits are acts or practices we so frequently repeat that they become almost automatic. Almost automatic means that I, the owner and manager of my habits and behaviors, have not given up control to them like some mindless robot. I use them as a tool or a convenience not unlike an automatic transmission, automatic bread-making machine, or automatic dishwasher.

I got into major financial trouble because I habitually repeated behaviors involving money, credit, and debt that produced enjoyable feelings and brought instant gratification. These activities were pleasurable because they blocked pain, masked fear, and filled desire.

At first glance that sounds like a pretty good method for coping, doesn't it? Don't kid yourself. Masking pain, anger, and fear by covering them with temporarily pleasurable feelings does nothing but make the masked emotions that much worse when the short-lived, pleasurable feelings wear off. And if that good feeling has had anything to do with credit cards and wild spending, a whole lot of guilt and anxiety gets mixed in.

The power of a habit

Habits can be learned and unlearned; bad habits, broken and good ones, established. Just think of the wonderful new behaviors we can unleash once we understand the power of a habit.

The secret to becoming a financially confident woman is this:

1. Investigate how financially confident women behave.

2. Eliminate habits based on false money beliefs.

3. Imitate and practice those positive and beneficial behaviors so frequently they become almost automatic.

Consciously identify those financial habits you desire to be almost-automatic responses in your life and then choose to repeat them frequently until they become almost automatic. That's the way to acquire good financial habits—or any kind of habit, for that matter.

Practically speaking, if you repeat a behavior twenty-one times in a row it will become a habit. Repeat it for an additional twenty-one consecutive times and you have the likelihood of a lifelong behavior. That means three weeks to establish a new habit if it is repeated on a daily basis, and another three weeks to make sure you've got it.

It can't be that easy!

It does sound simple doesn't it? If it were easy, we would've dumped our bad habits years ago, right? Well, perhaps. I'm the first to admit that just because I possess personal habits that happen to be bad and self-destructive doesn't mean I'm necessarily ready to get rid of them—easy or not. That's where the heartfelt desire to do the right thing comes in.

It's not like we haven't spent the better part of our lives making resolutions, promising ourselves to give this up, or start doing that. Only a fool would opt to hang onto bad habits if replacing them with good ones were easy. It's not always easy. Neither is most anything else that results in lasting value and lifelong positive change. Yet, it's worth the effort.

There was a time I secretly feared I had some kind of serious disorder—or at the very least, I was hopelessly addicted to spending money. It did seem rather appealing to blame something or someone for my bizarre behavior. Being a victim, after all, is quite fashionable these days and did offer an alternative to owning my problems. However, I finally came to this startling conclusion about myself: I behave the way I do because of my habits.

In the following chapters you're going to read about nine specific habits of a financially confident woman. These habits are very personal to me because I previously possessed none of them. These are the behaviors that have completely changed my life. Here's how I learned the secret of reprogramming my habits.

Dumping donuts

I've told you just about everything else about myself, so here goes with the donuts. I love 'em. I've always loved donuts. Donuts are fairly cheap, very available, and quite fattening. It's the fattening part that really made me want to break my daily habit. I should have been equally driven by the fact that I was spending a fortune at around a dollar a day. (Have you any idea what three hundred dollars a year will do when exposed to compounding interest?) But why do I really love donuts? They taste great. There's nothing like a high-fat, sugary donut to fill a nasty craving.

One day while listening to the talk radio, I heard my favorite psychologist, Dr. James Dobson, talk about this twenty-one-day habit-forming theory. It sounded pretty easy, and of course I was willing to try anything my favorite psychologist recommended. My donut habit seemed like it would make an excellent proving ground. I decided that for twenty-one days straight I would not eat a donut. Bingo! I'd be forever delivered from a terrible habit.

It wasn't quite that easy. The third day was the worst. That's when it dawned on me I was giving up my beloved donuts forever—not for just three weeks. I was obsessed and could think of nothing else but donuts. If my memory serves correctly, I lasted about five days and picked right up on that donut habit like I hadn't missed a beat.

I didn't blame Dr. Dobson. It certainly wasn't his fault I was weak and undisciplined. I was just thankful I hadn't told him or anyone else of my little experiment in trying to break a bad habit. I sure wouldn't want to fail out there where anyone could see me.

Quite a few years later I recalled the twenty-one-day formula and decided I would use it to establish a new habit rather than break an old one. I thought this tactic would have a greater potential success rate since it's easier to do something than not do something.

My second attempt to experience the miracle of twenty-one

involved my need to wear my car's seat belt (this was back before doing so was required by law in California where I live).

I know, this is something we should just do automatically. And it's not that I would consciously choose not to put it on; it's just that I wouldn't think about it, and my car didn't have an annoying warning buzzer or light.

After about a dozen days I noticed that my hand just went for the belt along with the chain of other movements required to get a car into motion.

After about three weeks, wearing my seat belt became a fairly automatic response; and after six weeks, I'd really made progress. It just didn't feel right to not wear it.

I successfully created a new habit that continued for some time. Until we changed cars.

The new seat belt didn't feel the same. The start-up routine was different. Before I knew it I repeated the not-belting act enough times (probably twenty-one) that the habit was unlearned. It was sometime later that I realized what had happened and I had to go through the relearning process all over again.

There are similar activities in your life that are so often repeated they've become nearly automatic. Take brushing your teeth for example. You do it so frequently and have for so many years that it is almost as automatic as breathing. And if we could capture this lovely behavior on video, I'm willing to bet you do it in the exact same way every time.

You pick up the brush with the same hand, open the toothpaste in precisely the same manner, start at the same place, and finish exactly the way you've done it for at least 365 times a year since those pearly whites poked their way into your tiny mouth. It's a habit.

Make a private list of your good habits. Not only will it be fun; seeing them on paper will be affirming.

Next, make a list of the habits you would like to establish. Don't go nuts with pages and pages of entries because that will only discourage you. It's hard to imagine I could live long enough to establish all the habits I could write down. Think of those be-haviors that are most important to you right now.

Perhaps it's your checking account monthly statement. If you are not in the habit of balancing that sucker every month, this would be a good time to make a personal commitment to break the habit of ignoring the monthly statement. Don't worry if you don't know how to reconcile the bank statement with your checkbook register, that's coming a few chapters from now.

In the case of a monthly activity, the theory says it will take twenty-one consecutive repetitions to establish the habit. But that's twenty-one months, you shriek. So? It's a worthy habit to get into, and I know you can do it.

Becoming accountable to another person is a powerful way to make a personal change. I don't mean that you need to shout it from the rooftops or publish it in the paper. Find someone whom you can trust to support you and stand by you in your desire to change. Your friend or buddy is not going to participate in changing you. That will never work. Yet, for some reason, the simple act of telling another person brings your personal com-mitment to a more conscious level. It becomes more important.

Tell that person you're setting out to consciously break a bad behavior by not doing it repeatedly until the practice is no longer almost automatic. Or tell your friend that you want to pick up a new behavior, and you will be repeating it until it be-comes almost automatic.

You might want to think about enlisting the help of a child in your quest to break a bad habit or develop a good habit. Let me assure you if you tell a young child that you want help in re-fraining from donuts you'll not only create for yourself a great reminder, you'll think long and hard before trying to sneak a donut when the little fellow's not looking.

Plot the calendar

As you think of breaking a bad habit or establishing a good one, twenty-one days, twenty-one weeks, or twenty-one months might seem like an insurmountable task. But remember your last birthday? And when is your next? Time really flies, doesn't it? Those twenty-one weeks or months (or years) will go quickly. They're going to go just as quickly if you begin establishing new behaviors or not. So you've nothing to lose but a bad habit and everything to gain, including a good one.

A calendar is a handy tool to help you visualize the birth of a habit. Mark on the calendar the starting date, the twenty-one points between, and the ending date. As you begin moving through the twenty-one repetitions, mark them off in an act of celebration as you move toward success.

Check your focus

I want you to know that I will never suggest you do something that I'm not willing to do myself. I know that some of the behaviors having to do with money are going to be great challenges for many, and I am facing a great challenge in the area of establishing habits even as I write. Changing behaviors starts with changing beliefs.

The next step is to consciously change your focus. We move in the direction of our focus, whatever it is. In the matter of finances, you must consciously decide to focus on positive money behaviors. The woman who successfully loses weight and goes on to become a weight-loss lecturer or counselor is a perfect example of how to stay focused.

When I began publishing my newsletter, *Debt-Proof Living,* which in the beginning went by the title *Cheapskate Monthly* (another shameless plug), I had no idea the fringe benefits I would receive from focusing on personal finance. I began the newsletter, quite frankly, in order to raise enough additional income to finish paying off our debts. I'd been fairly successful in changing destructive money behaviors, knew which techniques for getting out of debt and cutting expenses had worked for us, and wanted to share this information with others.

As you can well imagine, my daily focus changed almost overnight. In starting my new business my focus zeroed in on one topic: personal-finance management. In order to produce the best publication possible, my energy was channeled into research and communication.

Sixteen years later I realize that my personal progress has been significant because I've been constantly focused. Publishing *Debt-Proof Living* has done more for me than for any of its readers, I'm sure.

Had I focused on other areas and only delved into financial matters on an occasional basis, I'm quite certain we would not have made the financial progress we have. We're reaching goals we hadn't even considered setting.

Work in process

It's been several years now since I made a big decision to do something about my woefully out-of-shape condition.

It's not that I am not in excellent health. In fact, just the opposite is true: I have the world's most efficient metabolism.

I could be stranded in a desert for three, possibly four, years with nothing to eat and maintain my body weight. And with a little effort I'm sure I could actually gain a pound or two. My metabolism knows how to shut down so quickly and efficiently that giving up any body fat is unlikely.

Exercise has never been something of which I'm particularly fond. In fact I hate it, pure and simple. I've never been athletically inclined. With this in mind, even I was surprised when I joined a health club. I wasn't smart enough to join one where I would find others like myself sweatin' to the oldies. No, I joined the gym where Hercules and Miss Universe prepare for their next competitions.

It took about twenty-one sessions with Trainer Jose, (TJ) before my sessions became something even closely resembling routine. The first habit I had to establish was remembering to show up.

I won't even try to convince you that it was easy. It was very, very, very difficult. Everyone around me at the gym seemed to come by this weight-lifting thing naturally. Their well-cut, perfectly tanned bodies move in perfect grace and rhythm. I struggle with the most elementary routines, not unlike a baby elephant trying to get its balance.

Some time into my quest to fit in as a regular at the gym, TJ decided to switch my appointments to early morning rather than my usual evening schedule. I don't think I've had the opportunity to tell you that I was not born a morning person. How much of a morning person am I not? If forced to an upright position before the hour of 7:00 A.M. I have a pounding headache, queasy stomach, puffy face, crabby disposition, and overall defeatist attitude. I feel very sad and can cry at will. Believe me, it's not a pretty picture.

Twenty-one may be the miracle number for other habits, but to think it could make me do mornings was unbelievable. TJ assured me the morning schedule would be temporary. Even so, I kicked and screamed, whined and complained. The only reason I considered giving it a try was that my sessions for the following month had been prepaid. As precious as my sleep is to me, I preferred losing it to losing my money.

I made it to my 6:30 A.M. appointment several times. But as a happy person? One with the ability to say even one civil word? Not on your life. Just ask TJ, one of God's most patient creatures.

I was miserable and made everyone around me miserable. Working out in the morning became such an unpleasant and impossible expectation that I quit. I quit the gym and I quit TJ. Habits are all fine and good, but some things are just impossible.

I went three weeks with no workouts; and as God is my witness, the most incredible thing happened. I realized that going to the gym and working out under the strong (and I do mean strong) arm of TJ had become a habit. It just didn't feel right not to go. I missed it and began to feel miserable. I had this nagging sense that if I missed twenty-one times the misery would go away and I'd slip back into my old habits.

I rejoined the gym and gradually one morning at a time, over the course of years I have completely changed into a morning person.

Should you ever see me walking down the street, think kindly.

I will never have an athletic build, and I've just about decided that a thin one is not in my future, either. But I can curl some amazing poundage and am getting the hang of lunges and squats. I'm not half bad on the treadmill, and my resting heartbeat is becoming a much more respectable number. I've come a long way toward reaching my goal of being as physically active as possible until the moment God decides it's time for me to go.

Oh, by the way, since my original donut experiment, I've reapplied the formula to the problem. It worked. And continues to work now many years later. Not only have I not eaten a donut since I cannot remember, I don't even think about them anymore. And when I do, like right now, I really have no desire to break my habit. For me staying away from donuts is a good thing.

This technique can be used to establish new habits, such as balancing your checkbook, ceasing to use credit cards to create debt, establishing a daily skin care regimen, making your bed, or walking the dog.

In the coming chapters you are going to learn the minimum—the very least—that you need to know in every area of personal finance. You are not going to believe the transformation in your life as you begin to apply these twenty-one-day habit-forming techniques to each of these areas of money management.

Your Constant Companion

I am your constant companion.

I am your greatest helper or heaviest burden.

I will push you onward or drag you down to failure.

I am completely at your command.

I am managed with care—you must be firm with me. Show me exactly how you want something done, and after enough lessons, I will do it automatically.

I am the servant of all great people and, alas, of all failures.

Those who are great, I have made great.

Those who are failures, I have made failures.

I am not a machine, though I work with the precision of a machine and the intelligence of a person. You may run me for profit or run me for ruin—it makes no difference to me.

Take me, train me, and be firm with me, and I will place the world at your feet. Be easy with me and I will destroy you.

Who am I?

I am habit.

— Author Unknown

Chapter 6

The Least You Need to Know About Giving

"To tithe is to trust. It is to acknowledge that God will provide, that God will protect. When you give to God you create an investment in your own spirituality, your community, your family and your faith."
– Judith Briles, author, "Smart Money Moves for Women"

There are three kinds of women in the world: Those who take, those who give, and those who keep dividing the world into categories. Seriously, I have no statistics to support my contention, but it seems to me the takers outnumber the others by at least a million to one.

While a person's propensity to be a taker or a giver may be an inborn characteristic like any other personality trait, our society has certainly validated the takers—and possibly converted many of those prone to be natural-born givers as well.

Take credit cards for instance. My credit cards offered me entitlement—the right to possess goods and services up to, and often over, my allotted limit. To my mind, it seemed that the merchandise in stores was already mine, and I couldn't rest until I'd bought it and taken it home. The "have it all now" mentality has created a generation of takers, people who demand rights to which they feel entitled. No wonder this world is so out of whack.

Next time you have the distinct pleasure of vegging out in front of the TV for an evening, make a mental note of how many of the commercials have this underlying theme: You're entitled to take all you can get. If it's not a new luxury car that announces to the world who you are, it's a credit card that will guarantee you peace of mind and elevate you to a position of status you never thought possible. (How do they get away with such outrageous claims?) And the message commercial TV sends the kids of this country? It's frightening how subtly they are encouraged to get and take until their every little desire is fulfilled.

Learning to be a giver is probably the most important habit you can learn in your quest to become financially responsible. Being a generous person, one whose giving is so habitual it is almost automatic, will bring balance not only to your finances but also to your life. Giving provides the firm foundation upon which to build all the other habits we're going to erect.

I can't say I actually understand how giving works—how it is that in giving we receive. I don't understand how computers work either, but I've gotten into the habit of depending on the fact that they do. The work my computer so capably produces certainly makes me a believing non-understander. The same is true of giving. I don't understand it, but I believe in its power because the results have brought me indescribable joy and happiness.

There is something about the act of giving that cannot be explained in purely rational terms. I believe with all my heart that the act of giving invites God's supernatural intervention into our lives and our finances. I don't know about you, but the idea of opening my life to that kind of power is too awesome to miss.

Let me make this one thing perfectly clear: The attitude is not

I-give-so-I-can-get. No way! What could be more manipulative than giving ten bucks on Sunday because you desperately want a hundred on Friday?

Giving back to God a portion of what He's given to us is an act of worship, gratitude, and obedience. It's always been that way and it always will be. Anything more than a no-strings-attached, no-expectations manner of giving is manipulation, pure and simple.

The act of giving somehow escaped me as a kid. Sure I knew about the concept, but it was on a purely intellectual level. I didn't see the act for what it really was. I never caught the spirit of giving. Quite frankly, I figured God didn't really need my piddling amount of money. When I got really rich—when I got my finances straightened out—then I'd do some serious giving. I'd make a big splash with my philanthropic activities. What a dreadful, self-centered, self-serving attitude. But even with my arrogant attitude, God didn't stop loving me. He just waited patiently until I messed things up so badly it looked as if there were no way out.

In the truest sense of the word, I believe that by withholding what truly belonged to God I was in some way *stealing* from Him. Now that's a pretty horrible thought.

The very nature of grace is giving. God offers us grace, not because we deserve it or could possibly earn it, but simply because He loves us. Isn't it ironic that the credit card industry has picked up on this thing called *grace*? They offer what is known as a grace period. It's that time between a purchase and the time interest starts accruing. During the twenty-five days or so, grace is extended in the form of "no interest due." Grace—it is a beautiful thing.

I give to God because I love Him and because I am grateful beyond belief for all that He has done for me every day of my life. Giving from a grateful heart and expecting nothing in return is a sweet offering to the One who owns everything I have anyway. It's the very least I can do. And as I give I experience God's grace.

Do you have a secret little problem with greed? Give! Is it

tough to make the money last as long as the month? Give! Are you fearful of the future—afraid you will run out of resources, financial or otherwise? Give! Do you somehow feel your success and personal identity are tied to the balance in your checkbook? Give! When you are the neediest is when you should give the most.

How much should you give? Well, how much do you want to be blessed? You decide. Traditional thinking from ancient times until now says that ten percent is a good number. I like that and feel it is a good goal to set; but for heaven's sake, if you can't start with 10 percent, start with something.

Where should you give? Good question. You need to be a good steward of your gifts, so a bit of research on your part would be highly recommended. I suggest that if you are part of a church you should support it financially because that is the place where you are fed spiritually.

When considering other charitable organizations or ministries, first request a current financial report. Learn what they are doing, how they do it, and who is in charge. Personally, I am suspicious of any organization that is not open with financial affairs and one whose overhead and administrative costs exceed 25 percent. In other words, at least seventy-five cents of every dollar I give should make it to the cause to which I've donated.

If you've never been one to habitually give, get ready to experience a whole new dimension in your life. I don't know of anything that will take your eyes off your own situation faster than giving to others. I am so excited for you because I know what will happen in your life when you learn the habit of generosity. If you want your life to have purpose, your finances to come into balance, and your faith to increase, become a giver!

I would strongly suggest you add this to your personal belief system: *Part of everything I have is mine to give away. Giving is an expression of my gratitude, a drain for my greed, and the way I keep my life in balance.*

If you really believe that, your attitudes will begin to reflect it, your behavior will change, and your life will be greatly enriched.

You may be tempted to brush this belief aside thinking that in order to give you must have an independent source of money. Every woman, whether single, married, or divorced, has some money that comes into her life, something over which she has control. It may not be a lot and it may arrive sporadically, but the principle still applies.

I firmly believe that as we prove ourselves to be responsible with our resources, more and more resources will be entrusted to us to handle faithfully.

Quick tips

Even though giving is best done in secret, share with one other person, such as your spouse, a friend, or a mature child, about your commitment to giving.

Make giving your first bill. If you can't start with ten percent, start with five percent and increase it each month. Make payment coupons and place them in the front of your bills-to-be-paid file. Or add giving to the bills you have set up in auto bill pay.

Give away a percent age of your second most-treasured commodity: your time. Volunteer at a local shelter, food kitchen, hospital, or church. Visit several such organizations and ask God to direct you to the place your talents can best be utilized.

Be a responsible steward. Learn about the organization or individual who will be the recipient of your charitable contributions. Ask questions about how much of each dollar donated actually goes to the use for which it was received.

If giving doesn't immediately produce a burst of joy, don't worry and don't stop. Remember it's easier to act your way into a feeling than to feel your way into an action. If you wait for the feeling before you start being a giver, you may wait forever. Ask God to make you a cheerful giver. The joy will come, I promise.

Each day ask God to show you little ways you can be a giver, even if it's simply holding the door for another person or assisting someone with his or her struggles. Once you catch this whole attitude of giving, confrontations on the freeway cease to be confrontational, irritating sales clerks don't seem so obnoxious anymore, and daily chores like laundry and carpooling take on a different meaning.

Copy the following passage from Malachi 3:8-12 onto a card and post it where you can't help but read it every day.

"Should people cheat God? Yet you have cheated me! But you ask, 'What do you mean? When did we ever cheat you?' You have cheated me of the tithes and offerings due to me.

"You are under a curse, for your whole nation has been cheating me. Bring all the tithes into the storehouse so there will be enough food in my Temple. 'If you do,' says the LORD Almighty, 'I will open the windows of heaven for you. I will pour out a blessing so great you won't have enough room to take it in! Try it! Let me prove it to you!'

"Your crops will be abundant, for I will guard them from insects and disease. Your grapes will not shrivel before they are ripe," says the LORD Almighty.

"Then all nations will call you blessed, for your land will be such a delight," says the LORD Almighty."

I am so proud of you for the decision you've made to invite God's supernatural intervention into your life. God will honor His promises! Your step of faith will be rewarded. Just keep expressing your faith in this manner and giving will become a life-long habit.

Chapter 7

The Least You Need to Know about Saving

"The magic of compounding interest is truly the eighth wonder of the world!"
– Albert Einstein, philosopher scientist

Friends invited us for dinner one cold winter night, which where I live in California means you might want to grab a sweater.

The time of year and warm friendship blended perfectly with a dinner of homemade soup and honest-to-goodness homemade bread. I can say, without any doubt, that was the most delicious bread I've even eaten. I had to have the recipe.

I soon learned I would need more than the recipe—I needed "starter." The instructions were clear: You must feed the starter every three to five days, at which time you must also take out one cup of this weird-looking stuff to make bread.

It was fun at first, making homemade bread every three to five days. In a few weeks I became distracted and busy. I found the time to feed my starter but no time to make the bread. So I split and fed and ended up with two starters in the refrigerator. And then in five days I had to feed both of them, and remove one cup of the concoction from each starter and either make two batches of bread or do the split action again. My family of starters quickly began to take over the refrigerator.

Soon I became nearly obsessed with finding enough bowls and loaf pans to get all this bread baked because I didn't want to waste any of the precious starter. Visions of Lucy and Ethel in the chocolate factory kept coming to mind.

We had a lot of bread those first few weeks. But it wasn't long before it completely slipped my mind to feed my brood of hungry starters. You've probably already guessed the outcome. I killed 'em.

This "Friendship Bread" is a wonderful idea. The way it's supposed to work is this: You occasionally give a loaf of bread to a friend along with a supply of starter (there's plenty to go around, believe me) and the recipe, and that act of friendship starts the whole process of feeding, growing, baking, feeding, growing, baking in someone else's kitchen.

I calculate that about six months of this process, if followed impeccably, could fill every refrigerator in the northern hemisphere with the goofy-looking stuff that has the unique ability to make one feel terribly guilty for not baking bread every three to five days.

It is a lovely plan, provided you follow it. You have to give away the right amount, you have to feed it, and you have to make sure you never use it all. You must always leave some in the refrigerator to grow for the future.

Which leads me (you knew I'd get there sooner or later) to saving money. Both money and Friendship Bread require a delicate balancing act. You have to give some away, you must keep some to grow for the future (you dare not hoard the stuff), and you must use a good deal of it.

When it comes to finances, here's the bottom line: You can't keep it all, but you can't use it all either. The key is balance.

I have to tell you it makes me excited to know what's going to happen in your life once you're convinced that a savings program is something you must have. And personal confidence? You'll gain more than you could have ever imagined.

Correct distribution

Here is how your money should be dispersed—whether it's your own paycheck, the household income or sources of money than flow into your life:

- ♣ Pay God first.

- ♣ Pay yourself second.

- ♣ Pay others third.

Take all the time you need to pick yourself up off the floor. Yes, you read it right. God first, yourself second, and others third. That's just the opposite of the way most people handle their money, paying everyone under the sun first and then having nothing left for God or personal savings.

If the goal is to give 10 percent of everything to God, and it should be, why not dignify yourself with an equal portion? Ten percent is yours to keep. It sounds good, "Yours to keep." Not to save for a new sofa (saving is an excellent tactic for purchasing a new sofa, by the way), not to spend on next summer's vacation, but yours to keep. Yours to plant for the future. Yours to nourish and develop so that it will begin multiplying and working for you.

Fringe benefits

Saving money is its own reward. However, it has additional fringe benefits. Saving money is probably the best antidote for overspending. Saving money quiets the I have-to-have-every-thing-now monster that runs so many of us ragged. It settles our spirits because knowing we've done the financially responsible thing by not spending all of our resources has a calming, quieting effect.

Saving money will bolster your attitude and give you the strength and courage to face the temporary sacrifices that may be required to get your money life straightened out. You see, once you have put aside some money, even if it's a fairly small amount, cutting back on groceries or temporarily giving up your weekly nail appointment becomes a choice you make rather than a cruel mandate over which you have no control.

Three years before we were able to rid ourselves of leased cars, we discovered that my leased car with two years remaining on the contract was worth about the amount of the remaining lease. The idea of selling it, paying off the lease, and sharing one car between the two of us made economic sense. But even the thought was pretty tough for me to swallow. I'd had my own car since my early twenties, and I enjoyed the independence it gave me. I was nervous about giving that up and worried it would feel like failure, like we were losing ground rather than making financial progress. Being hung up on status symbols and impressing outsiders is not given up easily.

We kept talking about it, writing down the numbers, and projecting how such a move would bring us that much closer to being debt free. Carpooling to the office we share would present no problem. But what about my speaking schedule? One car would never do on those occasions when we needed to go in opposite directions.

We made the decision to sell the car, determined to try the one-car arrangement for awhile. If it didn't work, we'd deal with it when the time came. In the meantime we agreed that I would rent a car when I had a local speaking engagement.

That plan has worked very well for us. It's kind of nice to be chauffeured to work each morning, and I like driving a variety of brand-new cars when the need arises for a rental.

The best thing about the decision to go with one car after twenty-three years of having two between us was that we had a choice. By the time we made this car decision, we'd begun a regular saving and investing program. We began regularly putting away money that is growing for our future. We could've cashed something in or depleted an account to have the money to pay cash for a second car. Knowing we had choices made us willing to consider the most severe of the options.

But I know myself. If we'd had no money in the bank, giving up my car would have felt horrible, not like the choice that it was. It would have screamed "financial failure!" in my ears, and I'm afraid I would've done anything to not give up that car—including incurring new debt or some other defeating tactic. I would have looked at it as a husband-imposed repossession, and you know where that would've led—straight to resentment and disharmony.

The miracle of compounding interest

I guess you've already gathered that accounting and finance were never on my list of career considerations. Let me put that another way: Math makes me break out in a rash. Remember, I barely got out of beginning bookkeeping. I'll never know why I actually selected that class let alone stuck with it. I don't like to think about numbers, formulas, axioms, postulates, or anything that is even remotely related. Believe me, no one was happier than I with the invention of the personal calculator.

In spite of being numerically challenged, I find compounding interest fascinating. I'm in good company, too. Albert Einstein once declared the magic of compounding interest to be the eighth wonder of the world. And then there's Alvin Danenberg, another really smart guy who's also pretty wild about compounding interest. Al, a practicing periodontist and a registered investment advisor wrote a wonderful little book in language I not only understand but thoroughly enjoy (*21 1/2 Easy Steps to Financial Security*, by Alvin Danenberg, Publications International, 1995). Danenberg explains compounding interest this way:

> *In 1492 Christopher Columbus decided he was going to save for retirement. He had one penny ($0.01), and he knew he could earn 6 percent every year on his money. He put the penny in his left pocket and placed the inter-*

est ($0.01 x 6 % = $0.0006) into his right pocket for safe-keeping. He never added anything to his original penny in his left pocket. Yet, the interest accumulated year after year in his right pocket.

Chris is a very healthy guy: He lives until today—515 years later as I write—and decides to retire. So he takes his one penny from his left pocket and adds it to the simple interest in his right pocket. Do you know how much Mr. Columbus has?

Well, the interest in his right pocket added up to only $0.30 (515 years x $0.0006 = $0.30). Along with his original penny from his left pocket, he has $0.31 on which to retire. Not very good planning!

What could Chris have done differently? Let's assume Chris was much more astute about investing because he knew about compounding. Instead of putting the interest in his right pocket, he put it into his left pocket with the original penny—the principal. Over the years he would earn the same 6 percent interest on both the original penny and the accumulated interest in his left pocket.

As the story goes at the end of year one, he had $0.0106 in his left pocket (the original penny plus the 6 percent interest). At the end of year two he had $0.011236 ($0.0106 plus 6 percent interest). At the end of year three he had $0.01191 ($0.011236 plus 6 percent interest). This is called compounding and continued for Chris for 515 years. How much would good ol' Chris have finally accumulated for retirement?

The answer is somewhat more to Chris's liking. After 515 years of compounding the origial penny at 6 percent interest, Chris has $107,775,640,215.56. (that's 107 billion, 775 million, 640 thousand, 215 dollars and 56 cents). That's a lot of pocket change!

None of us will live that long, but all of us will have more than one penny to invest and will have the ability to compound our investments at higher rates of return.

When it comes to interest, compounding simply means earning interest on the principal and leaving that interest in the account to become part of the principal so that it starts earning interest, too.

There is nothing wrong with multiplying your assets by saving and investing. In fact, that is the sign of a wise steward who obeys God's financial principles. You might remember the story Jesus told in Matthew 25:14-30.

One of the characters in the story was given five talents to invest. He invested so well he multiplied the talents from five to ten. Another had two talents and doubled the value of his investment to four talents. However, the third took his one talent and buried it so it would be safe.

When the master of these three men returned he praised the first two employees for their wise multiplication through the investment of their resources. However, the third chap told the master he was fearful so he buried the money instead of putting it to work. The master called him a wicked, lazy steward who at the very least should have put the money in the bank where it could have earned interest.

Meet my fictional friends, Jennifer and Emily. They're both the same age, and in this illustration they are committed to saving $50 a month, which is $600 a year.

Jennifer is smart and starts saving at age twenty-one. She will save $600 a year for eight years ($600 x 8 years = $4,800) and then stop adding more, allowing her money to compound.

Emily, who is a procrastinator, takes eight years to get her act together. She doesn't begin saving $600 a year until she's thirty. But once she gets started she keeps adding $600 a year until she retires at age sixty-five. Emily contributes to her savings account a total of $22,200 ($600 x 37 years = $22,200) but cannot come close to catching up with Jennifer. The only difference in the way they saved? Jennifer started early.

Look at the chart on the following page to see the magic of compounding interest.

Pretty amazing, isn't it? I tell you this compounding interest

Age	Jennifer Saves	Total With Compounded Interest	Emily Saves	Total with Compounded Interest
21	$ 600	$ 600	0	
22	600	1,386	0	
23	600	2,185	0	
24	600	3,063	0	
25	600	4,029	0	
26	600	5,092	0	
27	600	6,262	0	
28	600	7,548	0	
29	0	8,303	$ 600	$ 600
30	0	9,133	600	1,386
31	0	10,046	600	2,185
32	0	11,051	600	3,063
33	0	12,156	600	4,029
34	0	13,372	600	5,092
35	0	14,709	600	6,262
36	0	16,179	600	7,548
37	0	17,798	600	8,962
38	0	19,578	600	10,519
39	0	21,535	600	12,231
40	0	23,689	600	14,114
41	0	26,057	600	16,185
42	0	28,663	600	18,464
43	0	31,529	600	20,970
44	0	34,683	600	23,727
45	0	38,151	600	26,760
46	0	41,964	600	30,096
47	0	46,160	600	33,765
48	0	50,777	600	37,802
49	0	55,854	600	42,242
50	0	61,440	600	47,126
51	0	67,584	600	52,499
52	0	74,342	600	58,409
53	0	81,776	600	64,910
54	0	89,954	600	72,061
55	0	98,950	600	79,927
56	0	108,845	600	88,580
57	0	119,729	600	98,098
58	0	131,702	600	108,568
59	0	144,872	600	120,085
60	0	159,360	600	132,745
61	0	175,296	600	146,689
62	0	192,825	600	162,018
63	0	212,108	600	178,880
64	0	233,319	600	197,428
65	0	256,650	600	217,830
Total	$ 4,800	$ 256,650	$ 22,200	$ 217,830

Note: Figures based upon 10 percent interest compounded annually. You will not find this rate in a savings account currently; however this is not unreasonable for money invested in mutual funds or other similar investments.

matter just never ceases to amaze me. Now let me amaze you a bit more. Let's say that Jennifer didn't stop her monthly $50 deposits at the end of eight years, and kept it up right to the day she retires at age 65. Her actual out-of-pocket contributions would have increased to a total of $27,000, but her account would have more than a half million dollars in it. Wow.

Let me also stress that the Jennifer and Emily story is for illustration purposes only to show you in black and white how compounding interest works. The illustration is based on compounding 10 percent interest. While at this writing there are no savings accounts or CDs paying that rate of interest, this example assumes the girls' money is invested in mutual funds or other type of investment.

Still, this story has a strong and power moral: Start early and feed your savings account regularly. Save as much as you can as soon as you can. The longer your money has to grow, the harder it will work for you and the more productive it will become. In our example Jennifer contributed only fifty dollars a month for eight years. Emily, who snoozed for those first eight years, had to contribute more than four times as much principal as Jennifer, and she still ended up behind at retirement by nearly $40,000.

How to get started saving

First you have to plan ahead. If saving a specific amount of money at a specific time each month or week is something you don't do presently, you have to learn to treat your savings commitment as you do your rent, mortgage payment, or telephone bill. As long as you see saving as optional, your chances for success will be so-so at best.

Let's say you decide to save one hundred dollars a month. To determine how much you need to save from each paycheck or other source of income, start with the annual amount (in our case it would be $100 x 12 = $1,200) and then divide by the number of times you are paid during a year. If you're paid monthly, it would be twelve times; weekly, fifty-two times; biweekly, twenty-six times; semimonthly, twenty-four times.

Here's a quick example of how much you would have to save from each paycheck in order to have a $100-a-month savings plan.

❖ If you are paid monthly: $100 from each paycheck

❖ If you are paid weekly: $23 from each weekly paycheck

❖ If you are paid biweekly: $46 from each paycheck

❖ If you are paid semimonthly: $50 from each paycheck

There's nothing magic about $100. It's simply a suggested place to start—and an amount that is easily within your reach.

Saving 10 percent of your income is the goal we're going to shoot for, and the closer you can come to that amount in the beginning, the sooner you'll reach it. The plan is for you to start saving and then increase the amount you save regularly until it reaches the optimum of 10 percent. If you can't handle $100 a month to begin? Make it less, but start somewhere. I suggest you make the amount just slightly more than what you think is comfortable. I want you to feel this the same way you feel it when you work out.

Let me point out that the saving we are talking about here is from your net take-home pay or household income. If you contribute to a retirement account like a 401(k) or 403(b), this savings is in addition to that amount. Here's why: You must have an emergency account, or what I call a Contingency Fund. If you are only contributing to a retirement account and you need that money because you are laid off or have a medical emergency, it will be very difficult—and expensive—to get your hands on that money. So think of your 401(k), 403(b), IRA or Roth IRA as money that is out of your reach for now. Your Contingency Fund is your stashed money that you manage and control.

Okay, back to building up a nice, big Contingency Fund. Make a commitment that whatever amount you select you will save that same amount at the same time every month and that you'll not decrease it if at all possible. And if you go through a season where you need to pull back, determine right now that you will get back to full savings as quickly as possible.

Find a Parking Place

You need to find a safe place to "park" your savings—a place that will be convenient, but not too convenient. However, let me make this really clear: Where you keep your savings is not nearly as important as growing a stash of money that you control. It is amazing how many adult Americans have absolutely no money in savings. If that describes you, don't be embarrassed: just be determined to change your status as soon as possible.

Investment or financial professionals would undoubtedly define "safe" a little differently than I. They would want your money safe from inflation and loss of interest. I want the same, but in addition I want your savings to be safe from you.

Look, I know how we are. I know that keeping my savings in my sock drawer is not safe because borrowing it back is all too easy. By safe I mean putting your savings in a place that is physically distant and downright inconvenient. I can't tell you the number of letters I've received that have recounted the same scenario: I started a savings account, but this or that came up and I had to use it. I want to help you prevent the temptation to take it back a little at a time until there's nothing left.

Local institutions

The first step to safety is to open an interest-bearing savings account at a bank or credit union. Most banks, even some credit unions, have a minimum deposit required to open an account. It might be $50 or more. And some charge fees and have other conditions. You want an account with no fees, no minimums and no conditions. They're out there; you just have to look. I suggest you start where you are most familiar—the place where you have your household bank account. Or go to that bank or credit union's website and read about the different kinds of accounts they offer.

These are typically the kind of accounts you will find at your bank or credit union:

❖ Passbook Savings

❖ NOW Accounts

❖ SuperNOW Accounts

❖ Money Market Accounts

❖ Certificates of Deposit (CDs)

Online savings accounts

Also known as an OSA, an online savings account is one that is managed and funded exclusively on the Internet through an online bank. OSAs are often characterized by high interest rates, which far surpass those of traditional savings accounts in banks and credit unions that have walk-in branches. By eliminating paperwork and reducing overhead costs, banks are able to pass the savings onto the customer.

Online savings accounts offer the yields (the amount you will earn through interest) that currently compare favorably with stocks and bonds, but also the liquidity of a savings account (meaning the cash is available to you at any time without the need to sell a stock or other investment) and the convenience to make deposits and withdrawals online. Most of these high-yield accounts have no fees, no minimum balance, and no lock-up period. Account holders may link their OSAs to their existing external bank accounts for easy transfer of funds between multiple accounts. Some also offer ATM cards so customers can directly access the funds in their OSAs.

There is a great website, *SavingsAccounts.com,* that keeps track of online savings banks and their currently-offered accounts, rates and contacts so you can make a comparison.

Savings coupons

Once you've determined the amount, frequency, and destination of your savings, you have to do one more thing—perhaps the most important of all. You have to make a commitment. What good is it to have a savings account and a good understanding of compounding interest if you don't ever get started. Are you going to be like Emily and wait for eight years to make consistent deposits?

Make out your own custom payment coupons, including the due date and minimum amount to be paid. If you will be depositing through the mail, make up a supply of stamped and addressed envelopes as well. Now is the time to create all the convenience you can think of. Keep these coupons and envelopes in the front of your bills-to-be-paid drawer. Once you have everything all ready to go, you won't be as likely to forget who's second in line to get paid. Exciting, isn't it?

Automatic savings

By far the easiest way to save money is to have it automatically deposited into savings before you ever see it. Automatic savings can be set up with your employer or with your own bank.

Here's how these savings programs work: You direct your employer or your bank to automatically withhold from your paycheck or withdraw from your checking account a specific amount of money. You might instruct your bank to transfer $50 from your checking account into your savings on the fifteenth of every month. The principle is: If you don't see it, you don't miss it. I know that sounds rather ridiculous, but it is absolutely true.

In a short period of time, you'll not only not miss the money, you'll often forget all about it. And when you get just a bit too comfortable with your savings contribution? It's probably time to increase the amount.

There is a reason and purpose for your savings. I will tell you about this in chapter 11 and also help you determine how much you need to accumulate in your savings account. For now it is important that you see saving as the second most important thing you do with your money. Giving is the first.

Ways to Raise Cash for Your Stash

Not everyone has a regular source of income or control over the family income. If this is true for you, making savings coupons or authorizing automatic deposits may not be possible at this time. So are you off the hook? No way! There are many other ways you can start saving. Here are some ideas to get your creative juices flowing.

Save all your change. This is probably the most painless way to sock away an additional couple hundred bucks each year. When going through the checkout stand, even if your bill comes to $4.12, don't break out the coins. Hand the clerk a five and you'll end up with eighty-eight cents in beautiful change to deposit into your change jar. When it gets full simply wrap the coins and make a savings deposit. My husband Harold taught me this trick. He can't stand to carry around change and has a change receptacle in the car, another in his desk, and still another on his bureau. His all-time best change year netted him $1,100, and those were after-tax dollars.

Keep a bank in the laundry room. The way I see it, she who does the laundry keeps the cash. How do those coins and bills make it through the wash and dry cycle, anyway? Unless your family is highly neglectful, your total take won't be much, but every little bit counts. I find at least $25 a year in the laundry.

Give up expensive habits. If you spend just $5 a day eating breakfast or lunch out, you're spending $1,270 a year and that's allowing for two weeks of vacation.

Eating at home or carrying your lunch two days a week will allow you to save at least $500 in the next twelve months. Imagine what you could save if you quit smoking, gave up lottery tickets, or cut back on other expensive habits you support.

Save all refunds and coupon savings. Instead of spending rebates and refund checks, save them. Take your grocery store coupon savings in cash: Next time you shop, ask the checker to give you the subtotal before coupons are deducted. Write your check for that amount and then ask for your coupon savings to be given to you in cash. Stash the cash in a special place or savings account, and you really will be saving money by using grocery coupons.

Hang on to windfalls. As you receive unexpected sums of money, such as gifts, bonuses, inheritances, retroactive pay, awards, and dividends, don't spend the cash—stash it. If you put those checks into your regular checking account they will just be absorbed into your everyday living expenses. Instead deposit them—no matter how small—into your savings program.

Keep making payments. As you pay off a credit card or other loan, keep making the same payments, but instead of sending them to the lender, put them into your savings account.

Sell assets. It's a pretty sure bet all of us have far more stuff than we really need or can possibly appreciate. Just think of everything you have to keep track of, protect, clean, store, insure, and worry about. What would you gain by unloading things that are robbing you of so much freedom? Sell! Liquidate! Give your savings program a jumpstart with the proceeds.

Chapter 8

The Least You Need
to Know About Debt

*"The poor are ruled by the rich, and those who borrow
are slaves of money lenders."*
– Proverbs 22:7

My first encounter with the word *debt* was in 1959. The Lord's Prayer—and its reference to forgiving debt—was part of the Get-Your-Way-Paid-to-Summer-Bible-Camp-by-Memorizing-Thousands-of-Verses Contest. Anyone who could successfully rattle off every single verse on the long list was awarded the coveted week at camp. To me, understanding the principle of debt in that context was about as pertinent as the drying time of paint. Qualifying for the trip was all that mattered.

I ran into a derivative of the word *debt* in my high school bookkeeping class. Mr. Black attempted to teach us the difference between debits and credits.

The theory of debt again crossed my mind (briefly) when I applied for a college student loan. A loan with payments deferred until some more convenient time in a far-off decade seemed so benign, so manageable. With my future at least four times longer than my past, why on earth would I let debt become of any concern at my tender age of eighteen?

By the time I hit thirty-something I'd experienced firsthand the phenomenon of being able to buy now and pay later, and quite frankly I'd found it to be neither easy nor something that brought satisfaction for any significant length of time. You might say I'd formed a love-hate relationship with consumer debt, and the love part was all but dead.

I allowed debt to creep into my life and wrap me in its tentacles. Believe me, it was trying its best to choke me to death. That's when I finally saw debt for what it truly is—a seemingly harmless little friend with a bent toward deceit and the unique ability to grow into an all-consuming monster.

Financially confident women do not feel prohibited from using credit, but I can assure you that they never think of debt as normal or commonplace. On the rare occasion they take on debt, it is well thought out and for a very short period of time, and they have a sure way to make full repayment.

True, credit has become quite commonplace in our modern society, and there is no doubt it's here to stay. The problem is that far too many of us have become strangled in our own credit lines. Debt has a unique ability to destroy wealth, damage relationships, and dispel joy when it ceases being a tool and becomes a noose with which we hang ourselves.

Three Kinds of Debt

All debt breaks down into three categories: Safe debt, stupid debt and survival debt.

Safe debt

Safe debts are those that involve collateral, also known as secured debts. Collateral, or security, is something that has at least as much value as the amount of money you wish to borrow, which you put up to guarantee your faithful performance.

The best example of a secured debt is your home. Your mortgage is a safe debt because you have pledged to the lender that if you are unable to make the payments, the collateral (the house and land) becomes the lender's. You car loan is collateralized by the car itself. If you don't make payments, the lender gets the car through repossession and you get to ride the bus. Safe debts typically have an require some kind of loan approval to determine if you can afford the payment on the secured debt.

Both you and the lender have a way to get out of the loan if you want. If you the borrower decide you can't make the payments, you can sell the collateral to pay off the lender or just hand the collateral over to the lender and call it even. Safe debt gives you a way out. The lender can sell the loan to another lender if he decides he wants out. Secured debts come with the the equivalent of a safety valve so you don't ruin your life.

Stupid debt

Stupid debt is debt you get on your signature alone without qualifying and without a wise professional considering for you if you can afford it. Stupid debt you get on an impulse. Stupid debt comes from allowing credit purchases to revolve on a credit-card account, opting to pay only the minimum monthly payment. It's the terrible reality of spending sprees and frivolous decisions. Stupid debt is the result of stupid thinking and stupid actions. It's just plain stupid.

Because it is not secured by collateral and you can get it on your signature alone, student debt falls into this category. I can't tell you how many letters I've received from women who are suffering under the heavy load of student debt. What puts student debt into this category is its lack of a safety valve. There is no way out, other than to pay off the loans in their entirety. Because there is no collateral involved, you have nothing to sell or to allow the lender to repossess.

Survival debt

This kind of debt is the result of paying for the groceries with credit and allowing that balance to roll from month to month, gathering with it large amounts of high-rate interest.

Payday loans, gaining popularity in many states have become one of the most common—and deadly—types of survival debt. Meant to be a very short term loan, a payday loan seems harmless at first. Nothing will sink your financial ship faster than getting sucked into the payday loan cycle where you'll pay from 390 to 780 percent interest and that's no typo.

Survival debt is the result of putting the rent on a credit card because the bonus didn't come through or the rent money went to repair the car or pay the utility bills or to buy clothes and diapers for the kids.

In 2003 consumers charged $50.6 billion in household expenses on VISA alone—for cable television, food, insurance, rent, mortgage payments and cell-phone use. And a 2005 survey revealed that seven out of ten consumers used their credit cards to pay for living expenses, medical bills, and car and home repairs.

Safe debt is manageable. Stupid debt is reversible because you can stop being stupid. But survival debt? Once you start paying for day-to-day expenses with credit because you don't have the cash for food or shelter you've crossed a serious threshold. Now you're caught in a vicious cycle.

You may believe you have no other choice but to keep adding to the gathering debt. But that's not true. You do have a choice. But you may need some major intervention to stop the out-of-control downward spiral.

Trying to manage survival debt is like trying to outrun an avalanche. You cannot run fast enough. You need to immediately get in touch with Consumer Credit Counseling Services (CCCS). You want to be sure you are dealing with a reputable and reliable organization (there are lots of look-alike credit counselors out there who are not legitimate; be sure you are dealing with a counseling organization that is accredited by the National Foundation for Credit Counseling). Call 800-388-2227 to be connected to the office closest to you. Or visit *NFCC.org* to learn more about credit counseling. These are people you can trust to tell you the truth and to lead you out of the dark night of survival debt.

The Trouble with Unsecured Debt

Easy to get

Never before in the history of this country has credit been so available and debt so attractive. A bank credit card is available to most anyone who can show as little as $10,000 annual income, which is just about anyone, including those on government assistance. While it is no longer lawful for credit card companies to send unsolicited credit cards through the mail, preapproved applications have become as common as any other type of junk mail. These applications can be as simple as a form requiring only a signature or as surreptitious as a large check made payable to the recipient that when endorsed activates a new line of credit complete with transaction fees, hefty interest rates, annual fees, and an instant monthly payment.

With an estimated ninety-five million American families in possession of more than 1.3 billion pieces of plastic on which they revolve $672 billion of credit-card debt, easy credit is more available than ever. Credit-card debt has soared, particularly among young people. Credit-card usage has tripled since 2001 amongst teenagers. Silly as the thought might be, the free prize packed in your kids' favorite breakfast cereal may turn out to be their first credit card—an idea that may not be all that far-fetched given the way credit is taking over our society.

The emergence of new players in the credit-card market means there's going to be more competition to retain you as a customer and to get you to sign up for new cards. You are a valuable commodity to credit card companies, but don't be too flattered. They have anything but your best interest in mind.

The average nonthinking person views an approved credit application as a badge of honor, a sign of having arrived, and concrete proof she or he is certainly able to handle this amount of debt. Nothing could be farther from the truth.

The credit card issuer sees you as a risk worth taking in order to increase their profit margins. They are banking on the fact that you will charge a decent amount of debt, habitually pay only the minimum monthly payment, and never be able to pay the balance in full. Fitting into that profile and operating according to their highest dreams and expectations makes you nothing more than a pawn on their chessboard of high finance.

Debt is expensive

Would you intentionally take more than thirteen years to pay back a $3,000 loan at 17 percent interest if it meant that you would end up paying more than $2,650 in interest alone for the privilege? Probably not. But that's what happens when you choose to make low minimum monthly payments offered by the typical revolving credit card. And the ugly truth is that few people run up a balance of $3,000 and then stop incurring new debt during those thirteen long years it takes to pay it off, one pathetic minimum monthly payment at a time.

Don't think for a moment that the credit card companies accept such a small portion of the actual amount owed each month out of the goodness of their hearts or as an act of friendship. They're no fools!

The amount you are required to pay as a minimum each month (usually about 4 percent of the outstanding balance) is actually the credit card company's profit—the interest you pay as a privilege of borrowing their money. If you pay off your entire balance each month, they've lost their golden-egg-laying goose. Ironically, cardholders who pay the entire balance in full and on time are known among industry insiders as "deadbeats" because they aren't paying their share of interest. That always makes me laugh when I think about it. Deadbeats!

The credit card companies make sure they get their money every month. By allowing you to roll the entire principal over to the following month, they're pretty much assured you'll stick with them for a long, long time. Perma-debt is what they call it, and that's what is supporting a mega billion dollar industry in this country—an industry growing by leaps and bounds.

At midyear 2001 the amount consumers owed on VISA, MasterCard, Discover, and the American Express Optima cards

crossed the $546 billion mark for a total credit card indebted-
ness of approximately $644 billion, representing a huge increase
over the past twelve months. Consumers have been going deeper
into debt at the rate of more than $5 billion per month or about
$173 million per day. As of January 2008, revolving consumer
debt hit $947,400,000,000 of which about $800,000,000,000
(zeroes added on purpose to bring home the "Yikes!" factor) is on
bank credit cards like VISA and MasterCard.

I don't know about you, but it's difficult for me to even think
in terms of billions of dollars. One of my *Debt-Proof Living* members sent in a bit of trivia that helped me understand the im-
mensity of a billion or even a trillion dollars, which is how we
now measure our national debt:

A dollar bill is about 0.0038 inch thick. A stack of one thousand bills is about 3 3/4 inches high. Ten thousand bills would
be 1 1/2 inches more than a yard high. A million would be 12.5
feet higher than a football field is long. A stack of a billion bills
would be 59.2 miles high, and a trillion would be 59,186 miles
high. Our national debt at $9.3 trillion would make a stack of
one-dollar bills 550,430 miles high! The moon is nominally
239,000 miles away, so our national debt in dollar bills is about
325,000 miles beyond the moon. The same analogy can be used
to visualize a person's personal debt. It takes $3,200 to make a
one-foot stack of dollar bills.

But wait—there's more! Just like the Ginsu-knife dealers, our
friendly credit-card companies have something special to throw
in, something designed to keep their finest customers loyal to
the bitter end (and yes, for many the end is very bitter).

For those who struggle along month after month and manage
to make their minimum credit-card payments on time, an award
is awaiting—a little something to brighten the spirits and lift the
soul: a credit-limit increase! And just as company executives
hope, most cardholders look upon that letter announcing the
increased amount of money available as a trophy suitable for
framing, proof of a job well done. Credit card companies absolutely love those who play the game according to their rules.

Geraldine, a divorced mom of three teenagers, works full-time
and has qualified for a $7,500 loan from her credit union. Get-

ting this loan will allow her to take care of some house mainte-
nance she's been putting off. It also will cover the cost of a
much-deserved vacation (a cruise sponsored by a ministry she
supports), and it will leave her with a little cash cushion in case
of emergency. She will be charged 16 percent interest over sixty
months, and her monthly payment will be $182.39. Given her
present financial situation she concludes that even though it
will be a stretch she will be able to cover the payment on her
present salary.

Unfortunately Geraldine made no further inquiries before
signing for the loan. The monthly payment was her only concern. But let's take a look at the full price tag—the real cost for
Geraldine to borrow this money. In addition to repaying the initial $7,500, Geraldine will have to pay $3,443 in interest for a
total repayment of $10,943. But that's not all. In order for
Geraldine to come up with the $10,943 necessary to repay the
loan she will have to earn considerably more because she will
pay the loan with after-tax dollars. You forgot about that, huh?
So did Geraldine.

In our example let's say Geraldine is in a 15 percent federal
tax bracket, must pay 7.65 percent Social Security/Medicare
taxes, and lives in a state with 7 percent state income tax.
That's a total of 29.65 percent that will be taken right off the
top of Geraldine's earnings. So in order to pay back the $10,943
in principal and interest, Geraldine will have to earn over
$15,565 in gross income. That is Geraldine's full price tag for a
$7,500 loan. More than twice the original loan amount. Amaz-
ing, isn't it?

A better alternative would be for Geraldine to force herself to
make $182.39 payments into the Bank of Geraldine before the
event, putting the money into an interest-bearing account for a
little over three years. That's how long it would take her to save
the $7,500 cash.

Debt is dangerous

Debt can be dangerous for your wealth, your marriage, your
relationships, and your peace of mind. It's not so hot for your

blood pressure, either. Statistics tell us that around 70 percent of all divorces found their roots in financial difficulty. I'm not saying that money troubles cause all divorces, but it's the money issues that get the conflicts going.

Over the years, I've received letters from people who are serving time for embezzling money from their employers. The stories are all so similar it's spooky. Invariably it goes like this:

The debts were so huge, the bill collectors so nasty, the family relationship so fragmented, I had to do something. I only took a small amount at first, but it was so easy. So I took a little more and it just got out of control.

I received a letter from a husband-and-wife team who were serving simultaneous sentences because they'd both become involved in breaking the law to deal with their debts.

The magnitude of debt

Debt is not a pleasant thing. Unsecured debt, like credit-card bills, installment loans, and personal loans, is the worst kind. At least if you buy a house, which is a secured or safe debt, and it turns out to be more than you can handle, you have the option of selling it, paying off the loan, and moving on to something else. Not so with unsecured debt. The very fact that the debt is unsecured means there is nothing of value being held to guarantee payment of the loan.

There was a time in my life that I regularly carried a very large and equally heavy handbag. So heavy was my bag, it turned out to be the cause of severe shoulder and neck problems. I've reformed in this area; and I now carry a tiny little thing just big enough for keys, lipstick, identification, and money. What a difference!

Carrying debt is a lot like my heavy handbag. It is cumbersome and a constant burden. Taking on additional debt would be like adding a shoulder bag, and then a backpack, and another bag for the other shoulder. Now if these heavy bags are debts, using a credit card to pay the credit-card bill would be equal to tucking three or four bricks into each bag.

Just picture yourself struggling through life, carrying all this weight. It's very difficult to get anywhere or make any progress, but the worst part is how difficult the journey is. Trying to stand upright with all this weight is nearly a full-time job. There's no time to look up and see the beauty, to experience the joy of the journey. While others who are less encumbered pass you by, you can't help but envy their ability to take side trips and excursions. But can you go? No way. You can't just dump the burdens in the trash or hope someone else will pick them up for you.

And when you pass through the struggles of life, such as sickness or unemployment, those debts don't magically disappear. They become heavier than ever. While it's hard to imagine, there are those (I know because I hear from and about them) whose debts become so unbearable suicide appears to be the only way out.

Debt destroys options

When burdened with debt you give up the option to quit a job in order to return to school. Or leave a miserable job to take one that pays less but would allow you to do something you truly love. Debt prevents us from following our dreams, or following our heart's desire to serve God in some profound way.

I'm reminded of the young woman who felt God was calling her to teach in a missionary school abroad. However, her debts were so large there was no way she could quit her present employment. She had no resources with which to pay the debts, and so she had to turn down the opportunity to go where she believed God was calling.

Each time you increase your debt you eliminate more options. The reverse is true, too. Each time you reduce your debt or pay another one off, you get back more options, until the day you are debt-free and your options are at an all-time high. That's what I call freedom!

Out of the debt trap

If you are one who is carrying heavy credit-card and other unsecured debt, I have good news for you. You can get out. And I have a plan for you called the Rapid Debt-Repayment Plan

(RDRP). It is the easiest and most efficient way to pay off all of your unsecured debt. It is simple and logical and really throws a monkey wrench in the credit card company's plans that you should stay in debt forever.

This is the way out of that trap.

1. Stop incurring new debts. If you keep spending on credit you will never be free of debt.

2. Get out all of your unsecured debts (credit cards, store charge cards, installment loans and personal loans) and add up the current minimum payments. This is the amount you must commit to pay every month until you are debt-free.

3. Arrange your debts according to the number of months left to pay until they will be paid in full. Put the one with the shortest term at the top. This order is critical because it provides for a big emotional pay-off as soon as you reach $0 on your first debt. And I want that to happen for you as soon as possible. Make your payments every month according to your customized plan.

4. When the first debt on your list reaches $0 balance, add its payment to the next debt in line. Repeat this process until you are debt-free.

The RDRP does not require an increased financial commitment. If you are able to make your minimum payments this month, you can do this plan.

Members of *Debt-Proof Living Online* (see page 225 to activate your free membership) have access to my Rapid Debt-Repayment Plan Calculator. It will do all the work for you, create your plan using the information you input and give you a payment plan you can print and hang on your refrigerator. You are going to get out of debt so fast, you'll be amazed.

First, look at the demonstration of the RDRP Calculator to see how it works. While it is possible to develop your RDRP manually using basic math skills, the calculator makes the process so much simpler.

Not only does this calculator do the math, it prepares your

complete plan right down to the last dollar. It shows you how your RDRP compares with the plan your credit card companies have for your future (remember they want you to stay in debt and support them forever) and the exact month and year you will be debt-free. All you do is plug in the exact information on your debts, press "Calculate" and then "Print."

But that's not all. You will be able to manage your RDRP on-line, one payment at a time ... one debt GONE at a time!

Project to one year from today. I can guarantee that you will not be the same person you are today. You will be either better off or worse off. Get busy becoming debt-free, and I can guarantee you'll be better off.

Chapter 9

The Least You Need to Know About Credit and Debit Cards

"Pay your balance in full every month by the due date, or else the card company can have its way with you. That's the only way to play."
— Bob Sullivan, author "Gotcha Capitalism"

They look alike in every way, but there is a big difference between your credit card and your debit card. And there are some hidden facts about both that are about to send you into a state of shock and awe.

First, what you know already: Using a credit card creates a short-term debt because you are borrowing money from the credit card issuer to cover the purchase. Using a debit card draws from your own money in your bank account.

It might seem obvious that by comparison a credit card is bad and a debit card is good. But don't be too quick to draw that conclusion.

Credit Card Basics

There are two ways that you can use a credit card: 1) as a useful tool or 2) as a noose to hang yourself.

A credit card is a useful tool if you pay off any balance that you might have during the grace period, which is a certain number of days between making the purchase and when interest begins to accrue.

A credit card becomes hazardous to your personal financial situation if you allow a balance to carry over from one month to the next, making only a partial or minimum payment.

Face it. We live in high-tech times. While ideal, it is not always possible to pay for things with cash. Nor is it advisable. Take an airline ticket, a rental car or an online purchase. These are not transactions that are friendly to cash. You need a credit card to pay in these cases. And you need to pay the bill in full before the due date so that you never carry a balance into the next month.

Only one

You need only one credit card. More than one will create financial chaos in your life. You do not need retailer credit cards. Just one good, all-purpose MasterCard or VISA (because they are accepted in the most places), that has at least a 25-day grace period and no annual fees.

If you return to $0 balance every month before the due date, you will be the winner in the game you play with your credit card issuing bank. Don't expect, however, to be named Customer of the Year, because they will not be happy with you. In fact, as I mentioned previously, in the privacy of their executive meetings they call you a "deadbeat," because you are not contributing to their profits. And that is exactly the way it should be.

As a bonus to paying off your balance each month, you will build a nice credit score to beat the credit card companies at their own game. This is ideal, and the state you should be striving to reach—if you are not there already. Remember, this is probably the only area of your life where being a deadbeat is a good thing.

Protected by law

The thing that makes credit cards an ideal consumer tool is the federal laws that regulate them. The Fair Credit Billing Act of 1974 is the law that has your back if your card is lost, stolen, or used without your permission or if something goes wrong with a purchase that you make with that card.

The law states that upon notification to the credit card provider that the card has been lost or stolen, you will not be responsible for more than $50 of any charges made by someone other than you. And most credit card issuers waive the $50, although by law they are not required to do this.

The law also gives consumers the right to dispute charges that are incorrect, or products or services that are unsatisfactory.

The downside

If you carry a balance from one month to the next, you are known in the industry as a "revolver." Now all the benefits shift from you and go to the credit card company. You've become your credit car company's slave and their "cash cow" because you willingly send them money every month. The credit card companies make the rules, and they change the rules at will.

To say that I've had a bit of experience with owning—and abusing—credit cards is like saying the Titanic sprung a leak. Thankfully, my ship didn't sink, although as you know, I came dangerously close.

For years as I was carrying and paying down huge sums of credit-card debt. I lived with the false security that if I absolutely had to use my cards again, I would rely on the grace period—the twenty-five or so interest-free days I would have to pay for the stuff I charged before the interest kicked in. That was my plan for how I would not add to my existing debt.

I cannot tell you how shocked I was to learn many years later that the grace period on all credit cards disappears the moment you carry a balance from one month to the next. I'm still surprised.

The vanishing grace period is not the only shocking fact about that deck of cards you carry in your wallet. There are more.

Low "teaser" rates

Credit card companies sent out approximately 5.3 billion offers for new credit cards in 2007—an effort that returned 32 million applications for new credit cards.

The competition for new customers is so fierce, credit card companies are constantly drumming up new marketing tactics to land new business.

Tempting low rates—even 0 percent interest—are a clever ploy to get you to respond to a company's offer. The plan is for you to transfer a balance from one card to another in hopes that you won't pay off the balance and will eventually pay a much higher rate once the teaser rate expires. Teaser rates are so slippery, it's difficult to hang on to them. Slip up and you could find yourself stuck with a big balance on a high-rate card.

Vanishing rewards

If you have a rewards card you may be earning air miles, vacation packages, discounts—perhaps even "cash back" as a percentage of what you rack up in charges.

Want to know what's shocking about your rewards program? The company can change the terms of the program—even cancel it together with the points or miles you have accumulated—without notice and for any reason. Credit card issuers are under no legal obligation to maintain the programs that they advertise. Shocking, I know.

Campus freebies

It's common knowledge that credit card companies go hard after our college students with free pizza, t-shirts and other trinkets as incentives to sign up for credit cards. What's shocking is that the schools are in on the deal. Universities and colleges are making millions by providing student, alumni and staff information to their partner credit card companies for direct mailings. Nearly every major university in the U.S. has a multi-million-dollar deal with a credit-card company, some having earned nearly $20 million while enabling young, unemployed students to plunge themselves deeply into debt.

Bait and switch

You pick up the mail and there it is—a 0 percent credit-card offer with no annual fee for the first year and no balance transfer fees. You can't sign fast enough, figuring you'll transfer your high-interest balances to this new card and then just pay it off really fast.

In the mail comes your new card. You waste no time transferring your higher-rate balance. Imagine the shock when your first statement arrives and you notice they charged a big 4 percent fee on the balance transfer, plus 17.99 percent on the entire new balance. What?! Where did your 0 percent go? You call customer service and are shocked to discover that your credit history and score didn't qualify for the original sweet deal you applied for. But by signing the application you unwittingly agreed to accept any substitute deal. Now you are stuck with a higher rate than you had before the switch—and the balance transfer fee, too.

Late fees

I hope you're sitting down for this one: In 2007 companies racked in $17.1 *billion* in punitive fees—late and over-limit fees. The average late fee was $33.64. Do this: Drop a $20, a $10, three $1s and 64 cents into the toilet. Flush. Imagine that.

It's shocking that so many people pay late, until you understand that a rising number of banks are setting unusual cutoff times like 11 a.m. rendering it virtually impossible to make your required payment on the due date.

If you think you can simply overnight your payment to guarantee it will be there on the due date, think again. credit card companies typically assign a different address for overnight deliveries, a fact they do not publicize. Send your payment to the wrong address, and you'll miss the deadline for sure. If the company can trick you into paying late a time or two, you'll lose your low interest rate and put a black eye on your credit score, too.

Over-limit fees

A spending limit on a credit-card account used to mean you could spend only up to that amount. If you tried to go over, the purchase would be denied. While embarrassing, a credit limit acted as a safety net. Well, don't look down now, but that safety net has all but vanished. If you charge over the limit, your issuer will gladly allow the transaction to go through. And then slap you with a fee of up to $39.

And if your next payment doesn't cover the fee, plus enough to get that principal balance back down below limit, you'll get slapped again next month. And the next.

Miserable miscellany

Credit card issuers are finding new ways to squeeze fees from customers who pay their balance in full every month, too. In fact, they may have added a new one since you began reading this chapter.

Many banks now charge a fee of $10 or more if you choose to pay by phone. Need a copy of a past billing statement? It will cost you $2 to $13 per item. And should you need a rush delivery of a credit card, prepare to fork over a fee of up to $20.

Going up, and up

This is really going to shock you: There is no limit on how high banks can raise the interest rates on credit cards. Interest rates are subject to the laws of the state in which the issuer has credit card operations. Now you know why most card companies are located in either South Dakota or Delaware. Neither state has caps on rates.

Even if your credit card has a "fixed" rate, don't get too comfortable. Remember you signed an agreement that gives the bank permission to change the terms of your agreement "at any time and for any reason." All credit-card applications carry this catch-all provision. Federal law requires that you receive at least 15-days' notice of changes to your account. Keep your eyes open because this notice will likely arrive as a scrap of paper with your statement or as a separate piece of mail that looks just like junk.

Multiple rates

If you look carefully at your credit-card account you will see several interest rates. There's one for balance transfers, another for new purchases and yet another rate for cash advances. Now look in the fine print.

You will find a clause that states the credit card company can apply your payments in any manner they desire. Here's an example. You carry a balance of $2,000 at 11.99 percent. You need $500 fast. Payday is a week away, so you take a cash advance for the $500, knowing you'll pay a 3 percent cash-advance fee.

Even at the outrageous rate of 27.99 percent for cash advances, you figure it won't be that much because you will pay it back in a flash. Oh, you are so wrong.

When you make that $500 payment, you cannot elect to have it apply to the $500 now accruing at 27.99 percent interest. The bank will apply it to the lower interest rate balance, leaving that $500 to run up a lot of interest at the higher rate. Only when you have paid the $2,000 portion of your account will your payments begin to pay down the higher rate balance.

Universal default

There is a clause in your agreement that says basically if you are more than 30 days late on any payment to any creditor, the interest rate on any credit card could shoot up and your credit score may be damaged. There has been such an outcry from consumer groups against this unfair practice, that several of the credit card issuers have stopped exercising their rights to universal default. But don't get too excited. Until credit card issuers remove the clause that allows them to change the terms at any time and for any reason, what they say today can easily change tomorrow. And probably will.

It should come as no shock that credit cards are not as simple as they used to be. And learning the truth about what's buried in the fine print of our agreements is the best way to avoid the pitfalls that can cause us to stumble.

Debit Card Basics

Every debit card these days has either a VISA or MasterCard logo on it, which makes it look like a credit card in every way. But looks are where the similarities end.

Nothing to do with credit

A debit card is NOT a credit card, cannot work like a credit card and has absolutely nothing to do with credit. Using a debit card responsibly will not improve your credit score. Using it flawlessly will not be reported to the credit bureaus.

Most debit card holders falsely believe that they simply cannot get into financial trouble if they only use a debit card because "the money comes straight out of my checking account!" They believe they are safe because they cannot spend money they do not have.

Two ways a debit card works

If you have a debit card with a VISA or MasterCard logo on it (VISA calls it both an ATM card and a VISA Check Card, MasterCard calls is a MasterMoney Card) there are two types of transactions that you can make with it:

1. Debit where you are required to input your PIN, which is also called an "online debit."

2. Credit where you must add your signature, which is also called a "signature debit" or "offline debit."

This is very confusing, so let's take it just one step at a time.

When you pull out your VISA or MasterCard debit card to pay for your purchase, the clerk will ask "debit or credit?" (Remember, it *looks* exactly like a credit card so the clerk has no idea which yours is.) When you are using a debit card and you reply "debit" to the clerk, it becomes a PIN-based transaction. You are required to enter your Personal Identification Number (PIN) after the card has been swiped through a point of sale (POS) terminal.

With PIN-based debit card transactions, funds are withdrawn from your checking account immediately at the time of the transaction.

When you reply "credit" to the clerk, it becomes a signature-based transaction. Signature transactions do not require your PIN, but you must sign a slip to accept the transaction. With signature transactions, funds are held in your checking account at the time of purchase until the transaction posts to your account in one to three days.

The only thing a signature-based transaction (the one that happens if you reply "credit" when using a debit card) has to do with credit is that *it is processed in the same batch of transactions as those made with credit cards.*

More merchants have credit card readers than PIN-based readers and banks make more money when you use an offline debit card than when you make a PIN-based online transaction (the bank gets a percentage fee, or merchant discount, from the merchant who accepts the offline card, instead of a smaller flat fee for PIN-based transactions).

That's why banks push so hard to get you to accept one of these debit cards in place of your old ATM card. (They often send them and instruct you to stop using the old ATM card that is no longer valid, making it appear that you have no choice but to accept a new debit card.)

For either debit card transaction, both banks and merchants make more money and face lower risks than when you write a check—the bank saves money on check clearing costs, there is less float time, and the merchant doesn't need to worry about bounced check risks or bounced check fees.

Again, and I want to be perfectly clear on this: *Debit cards have absolutely nothing to do with credit, even though the system uses the word "credit" to indicate which way you wish your debit card transaction to be processed.*

Overdrafts by design

Banks now allow customers to overdraft their accounts using their debit cards at checkout as well as at an ATM. This is a new trend and one you need to understand fully.

Even though your bank has the ability to stop you from swiping your debit card to pay for a $5 hamburger when you have only $4.94 in your account by declining the purchase—they don't. Banks now allow the purchase, citing "convenience for the customer" or saying they don't want to embarrass or interrupt the flow of life for you, their valued customer. But they are also gleefully slapping you with a huge penalty if you do not have an overdraft protection account (something altogether different, wherein credit is attached to your checking account—with fees and charges, too), or you have not arranged to have your savings account tapped when you inadvertently go over.

And this practice has become widespread. Banks have discovered the enormity of this new income stream of penalty fees. In 2005 approximately 46 percent of all bank overdrafts were triggered by debit card transactions or ATM withdrawals, while paper checks triggered 27 percent of overdrafts. Banks collected $17.5 *billion* in overdraft fees in 2005 alone.

Debit card POS (point-of-sale) overdraft loans are more expensive than overdraft loans from any other source, including overdrafts by check. Debit card POS overdrafts cost debit card users $2.17 in fees for every dollar borrowed, compared to check overdrafts, which cost eighty-six cents per dollar borrowed.

The EFTA

Debit cards are regulated by what I consider to be a fairly weak law, The Electronics Fund Transfer Act (EFTA). It states in part that if your debit card is stolen and funds removed from your checking account by a thief, you must report this to your bank within two days.

Okay, tell me how many of you balance your checking account every two days? Most people don't balance it monthly when the statement arrives. But if you do not notice and report a discrepancy in your account in that time frame, you are liable for up to $500 of the theft. And if you do not report it within sixty days, you may be liable for the entire amount.

VISA and MasterCard often use this situation as a marketing tool as well, announcing in dramatic commercials that if someone steals money from your account using your debit card, they will restore every penny of it—no questions asked. Well good for them, but don't be hoodwinked. They can change that policy anytime. They are not bound by federal law the way they are when they issue credit cards but you are not likely to know for sure until you have a problem. (Remember the Fair Credit Billing Act? It only covers credit cards, not debit cards.)

The EFTA has other provisions that protect the bank more than the debit-card holder. If the bank decides that the reason the thievery occurred was because you were negligent with the card or handled it in such a way that gave access to a thief, they can choose to not cover any of the burglary of your funds.

The EFTA gives the bank or credit union a lot of discretion for how they can handle your situation.

No consumer protection

Let's say you buy something over the Internet with your debit card. That widget never shows up—or it shows up broken. Or it's not the correct item you bought, or you have a problem getting a refund. Since you paid with a debit card you are on your own because the money has been withdrawn from your account. There is no credit involved here, so you have none of the protection afforded you by the federal laws that regulate credit cards. You are out the money when you use a debit card.

Or let's say you're going on a cruise and you pay for it on your debit card. The cruise company files bankruptcy only weeks before you're to sail. Can you get your money back? Not a chance. But if you'd paid with a credit card, no problem. The issuing bank has to eat the loss—not you. It's the law.

A horror story

Do not assume you'll never have a problem with your debit card getting into the wrong hands, (remember only the card number is needed to buy things online—no PIN or signature required). A thief who has a copy of a debit-card restaurant receipt for example, can drain your checking account, even if the card itself or PIN hasn't been stolen. Consider the story of one of my DPL members:

Late on the Friday after Thanksgiving a stranger went shopping online with Carol's debit card. To this day she does not know how he got the number, but that's all he needed. He didn't need a PIN or any kind of identification to shop his brains out at Target's online store. He spent thousands of dollars on Christmas gifts—all paid for with Carol's debit card.

It was more than a week before Carol figured out what had happened. When the bank called to tell her she was overdrawn she was horrified. She knew for certain that she had quite a bit of money in her accounts.

After many terrible hours that included making a police report, it was discovered that someone other than herself had done a lot of Christmas shopping on a holiday weekend when discovery would not be quite as likely. That thief was right. Not only did he clean out her checking account, when it became overdrawn the bank automatically tapped into her savings accounts. Only when everything was gone did they contact her.

The bank tried to be understanding, but they had no way of knowing if Carol had really authorized these charges. They even suspected that she really made the charges herself. Eventually they agreed to investigate, but big deal. She was broke through the holidays while the bank moved at its own pace to find if there was a problem. Finally after many months, the bank agreed to restore some of the money that was stolen, but not nearly all of it. Carol came out a big loser.

My advice to you: When shopping online and by mail order, never use a debit card. The risks are just too great. Pay with a credit card and you will have the muscle of federal law to protect you against would-be thieves.

Infuriating blocks

Did you know that every time you use a debit card at a gasoline filling station, a chunk of your checking account can be blocked—sometimes for days, with the potential to cause you all sorts of financial headaches and bounced checks? It's true. The same holds true for when you rent a car or reserve a hotel room using a debit card.

If you use your debit card at a gasoline pump that does not require a PIN, your bank regularly will block out an amount—up to $75 on your card. But you will not be told about this. So when you continue shopping and bring your balance below $75, wham! Another overdraft fee, which could be up to $40 per infraction if you do not have overdraft protection. Sadly your bank is giddy with joy each time this happens, because you are contributing to their income stream and profit margin.

Money leaking all over the place

You will spend more. It just gets my goat when I think of how much MasterCard and VISA have spent to brainwash Americans into thinking they are more responsible if they use a debit card in their daily spending. That is by design.

The big two declared four years ago that they'd successfully trained Americans to use credit cards for their larger purchases, but now they wanted to get involved in all the smaller purchases, which people make with cash and paper checks. They've done a good job of it.

But, you may ask, what's in it for them since the money comes straight out of my checking account? Oh, let me count their benefits.

First, it is proven that you will spend more when you shop knowing you will simply swipe your debit card rather than pay with cash. In effect you have the entire contents of your bank account available in your debit card. Sure you only intend to spend $20 in the drugstore, but if you happen to go over that, it won't matter. Right?

In fact I once read a VISA marketing brochure for merchants that stated average sales will improve by 200 percent when you begin to accept debit cards and place a PIN machine at the checkout. Two hundred percent! No wonder merchants are quite anxious for you to shop with plastic.

Cash rules

Cash is not necessarily dangerous or unsafe, but it is inconvenient and that's a good thing. You have to plan ahead; you have to stop by the ATM to get the cash before you go to the store. And that's even better because it forces you to notice how much you are spending. Pulling $20 bills from your wallet requires you to engage your brain and forces you to consider how much you are spending.

Chapter 10

The Least You Need to Know about Living Below Your Means

"Living beneath your means is the only route to take to enjoy a secure and comfortable standard of living throughout your working and retirement years. Living beneath your means isn't a suggestion. It's an imperative. Spend less than you earn!"
— Jonathan D. Pond, author, "1001 Ways to Cut Your Expenses"

I was repulsed by the word until I understood it. Frugality is just doing whatever it takes to spend less than you earn. Another way to put that is "live below your means."

What a novel concept.

Frugal doesn't mean tacky, frumpy or stingy. It means we don't spend money we do not have yet.

The truth is I am a cheapskate. Okay, don't panic. This is good. It's the difference between what I used to be (a total credit card junkee) and who I am today.

In a nutshell this is what happened: I made a commitment to stop spending before we earned it. I stopped making calculated and arrogant presumptions on God's mercy. I stopped assuming he's going to bless us in the future with a paycheck, spending it now, and then hoping and praying he pulls through.

Contrary to the picture you may have in your mind, I don't live in a shack in the woods, foraging berries and grubs for dinner. But I do fix stuff instead of running out to buy new stuff. Another novel concept. I figure out how to use this for that when that costs more than this. We drive paid-for cars; we challenge everything and ask if there's a better way before spending money.

Frugality is not about pinching every penny until it screams. It's about making calculated choices that lead to freedom. It's about trying different things until you find what works for you and that allows you to live the best life you can without depending on credit. The payoff is that soon you don't have to worry about making ends meet or juggling the bills in hopes you might be able to get them all paid before they start arriving again. It's about having the money to do and have the things that really matter to you.

Here's an example: I used to get my hair cut every four weeks. Then I figured how to stretch that to six. That's four-and-a-half fewer haircuts a year, which translates to, well, you do the math. Apply this kind of thinking to all areas of spending and just watch the dramatic results. Being a cheapskate is less embarrassing than you'd think. Unless you count that half haircut. Ha.

The secret of simplifying

Any woman with a lick of fashion sense knows the secret of style is found in three little words: accessorize, accessorize, accessorize.

Men have it easy when it comes to accessories. All they have to worry about is a tie, a watch, a belt, and maybe a briefcase. Their shoes don't really count as accessories because they're almost always the same color and height.

But women? We have to deal with earrings, watches, bracelets, rings, necklaces, belts, chains, broaches, scarves, glasses, stockings, socks, rings, hair ties, clips and bows, headbands, handbags, briefcases, and shoes of every style, height, and color. Being properly accessorized is anything but cheap. Or easy.

First it's a matter of finding suitable storage space. Now I've observed individuals who appear to be wearing every accessory they own, but we usually need lots of space to store all the accessories not currently in use. And that just screams for some type of time-consuming, fancy organizational system because, as they say, if you can't find it, why have it? Or as I used to say, if you can't find it, replace it.

However, in an amazing fit of sensibility several years ago when I discovered the loss of yet another piece of ear jewelry, I made a rash decision. I would own just one all-purpose, lovely pair of earrings. I would wear them all the time. Period.

Why not? I thought. I wear the same ring day after day, year after year, and have not yet been arrested for taking unacceptable fashion risks.

At the time, I didn't realize what a brilliant decision this was. This small change simplified my life immeasurably. I've saved all kinds of time not having to decide which earrings to wear. And even more time not having to locate two that make a reasonable match. Because I always knew the exact location of my one pair of earrings, I hung onto that single pair for many years. Eventually one earring broke, which required a replacement. And I received a pair for a gift so I have several pair now, but nothing like the amount of earwear I once managed.

Ironically, this idea born out of a desire to stop spending so much money on earrings has produced an even more desirable fringe benefit. Simplifying, even in the tiniest ways, makes my life more enjoyable. Simplifying helps reverse the process of being overpowered, overextended, overworked, and overcome by the pressures of life—pressures that are mostly self-imposed.

Simplifying, even when done in a tiny way, has the ability to refresh the soul. You won't believe all the extra time and freedom you'll enjoy, to say nothing of the positive effect on your bank account.

Living simply doesn't mean moving back to the land, ditching your favorite appliances and slaughtering your own meat—unless of course that's your idea of simplicity. Simplifying means getting by with less, while maintaining comfort, eliminating complexity whenever possible, and minimizing the time demands that have a way of devouring us.

Here are three examples of ways to simplify that won't impact your life negatively:

❖ **Stop buying clothes that need to be dry-cleaned.** Maybe you prefer to spend fifteen to twenty dollars a week running to the dry cleaners, but just consider the expensive waste of time it represents.

❖ **Make water your beverage of choice.** Just think of all the cans, jars and bottles you won't have to buy, lug home, and then lug back to the recycling center.

❖ **Sell the stuff.** If you've reached the point where you no longer believe the bumper sticker, "He who dies with the most toys wins," it's time to start unloading. Author Don Aslett in his book, *Clutter's Last Stand,* hits it right on the head when he says, *"Dejunking is the cheapest, fastest and most effective way to become physically and financially sound, emotionally and intellectually happy."'*

Spend less to save more

There's only one way to accumulate money. You must have more money coming in than going out. You have to make more money than you spend. You must spend less money than you make. This is a simple principle, and those who live according to it know the result of spending less than you earn is financial security. If you spend it all, there will be nothing left over. And if you spend more than you earn, you're on the road to trouble with a capital T.

Affluent people are those who earn money and manage to hang onto it by spending less than they make. Frugality is one thing that separates the affluent from the rest of us.

Perhaps the terms frugality and thrift cause you to grimace.

I know that's how they affected me. The words meant nothing short of purchasing my entire wardrobe at a thrift store. No way was I ever going to buy my clothes at the thrift store, a promise I made to myself at age eleven. Guess that tells you where many of my clothes came from.

I plead with you to give up your biased ideas of what frugality means. Just give it a chance. I believe you may come to learn that being frugal and living with thrift in mind are actually virtuous characteristics. You need not fear becoming one big fashion disaster or less classy and dignified than you are right now. I have confidence in you.

When you think about it, there is little we actually need—that is, really need in order to sustain life. These needs of course would be shelter, food, and clothing. These things are absolutely essential to sustain life. The next level of expenses are certain comforts we've come to enjoy and want in our lives. And finally there are luxuries, those things in which we indulge to pamper ourselves.

The ideal way that our finances should be distributed is this: 10 percent to be given away, 10 percent to be saved, 80 percent to live on—to cover essentials, comforts, and luxuries. Not easy if you've been used to living on 100 percent, or more, giving little (if any) and saving nothing.

Frugality simply means striving to get the very best value you can for each dollar and fully enjoying the things you have or make use of.

Frugality is not an activity reserved for the poor and underprivileged. Instead it is a noble way of life that is to be admired. Frugality is the mark of a good steward, one who is pleasing to God. To approach life with a mind toward frugality is to celebrate life, to surround oneself with beauty, and to be content. Living a life of frugality offers a giant sigh of relief to those of us used to overconsuming and under enjoying.

We are so wasteful of the abundance that comes into our lives and our homes. Right living means using things up, wearing them out, and even doing without now and again. To be frugal means to have a high joy-to-stuff ratio. It means balance—not having too much or too little but just the right amount.

Think of all the stuff in your life, a great deal of which you probably haven't used or even thought about in years. If it isn't truly useful or doesn't bring beauty and joy to your life, why have it? Think of all the things that take up your time and energy because they need to be dusted, polished, fueled, mowed, insured, secured, and fussed over.

There's something refreshing about simplifying, about knowing when enough is enough. Both the Old Testament, *"Don't let me be too poor or too rich. Give me just what I need"* (Proverbs 30:8), and Jesus when he said *"You cannot serve both God and money"* (Matthew 6:24), challenge our culture's adage that more is better and you better get all you can right now.

Cut back in every area

The key to reducing is to look at the whole picture. You probably do not need to eliminate one area entirely, but rather cut back a little bit in every area.

Once you've kept a written spending record (chapter 13) for one or two months, you will have no problem seeing where the money goes. And you will know instinctively where the cuts need to be made.

As you look at your first full month of recorded spending, play with the figures a little bit. Muster all the courage you can and multiply some or all of them by twelve. It's good to see what you will spend on fast food, for example, if you continue spending at your current rate. Or the telephone bill. We fool ourselves by never thinking about total annual costs. Spending sixty dollars a month for telephone service may not seem like much, but that's $720 in one year. If you could reduce that bill by 30 percent (not difficult if you apply all the cost-cutting techniques available) you will realize a $240 savings in a one-year period. That's remarkable.

By now you've rethought your values, particularly those related to money. Focus on what you've determined is really important in your life and the lives of your family members. We get so caught up in our lifestyles we fail to realize we're spending a great deal of our money on things that don't even fit into our value system.

Seventy-Seven Ways to Spend Less Money

Here are a few tips for simplification that might work for you. Perhaps they'll help you think of other ways you can slow down and enjoy the things that really matter.

General

1. Give up the myth. Myth: Buying things on sale is a great way to save money. Truth: Buying things on sale is a way to spend less money, but it has absolutely nothing to do with saving money.

2. Stop trying to impress other people. If you can stop spending according to demands put on your life by others (through peer pressure or the necessity to keep up), you will see a tremendous difference in the way you spend.

3. Stop shopping. To me, shopping means strolling through the mall with nothing particular in mind, simply looking for great bargains and things that happen to strike my fancy. That is a very dangerous thing to do. I'm not suggesting that you never buy anything again, but that your spending should become a planned act of acquiring the goods and services you need, not spur-of-the-moment, impulsive spending.

4. Anticipate. There's nothing more frustrating than waking up in the morning to a water heater gushing forth water from a rusted-out bottom or a flat tire with the steel belts exposed. You have no choice but to replace them immediately. Now, had you anticipated the tire was about shot or the age of the water heater meant you were on borrowed time, you could have watched for sales and had time to comparison shop. But you've no choice but to get whatever you can by any means possible. And you will invariably spend a great deal more, especially if you have to make that purchase on credit.

5. Purchase with cash. Retailers are keenly aware of the statistics that prove you will spend at least 30 percent more if you are in the store with a credit card, debit card, or checkbook. The last thing they want is a customer who carries cash. Why? Because they know how cautious and non impulsive the cash buyer is.

6. Keep a spending record. Seeing where your money goes keeps you from lapsing into a spending coma.

7. Save first, spend later. Instead of putting larger purchases on credit, save first. Once you have enough cash, make the purchase. Amazingly, by the time you save up the money, you may change your mind a dozen times. You might even decide you no longer need or want it.

8. Combine errands. Instead of running all over town several days a week, combine all your errands into one trip.

9. Use baking soda. It's cheap. As a non-abrasive scouring powder, it cleans and shines chrome, unclogs drains, removes hard-water marks, cleans plastic, removes odors, degreases, removes stains from marble, cleans fiberglass, removes crayon stains from washable walls, and when added (1/2 cup per load) to laundry with liquid detergent it greatly improves effectiveness.

Cars

10. Reassess transportation. Perhaps you don't really need more than one vehicle. Many cities have lovely public transportation facilities. Have you tried yours lately?

11. Cheapest gas. It takes only a few seconds to log on to *GasBuddy.com* to find the cheapest gas in your neighborhood the day you need to fill up.

12. Do it yourself. Take a course in basic auto repair to learn how to change your oil, oil filter, and antifreeze. Learn to spot a hose that needs to be replaced and detect the origin of a fluid leak.

13. Buy, don't lease. Generally speaking, leasing a new car is the most expensive way to go. Better: Purchase a late-model used car. The major depreciation of the car will have occurred during its first year when someone else owned it.

14. Keep your tires filled. Check them weekly to make sure they're impeccably inflated, holding exactly the amount of air pressure as recommended on the sidewall of the tire. You should be able to increase gas mileage by up to 10 percent.

15. Keep your trunk empty. The more weight you're hauling around, the fewer miles per gallon you'll get from your fuel. So unload all that heavy stuff you've been carrying around. For the best performance limit your trunk's contents to the necessary safety emergency equipment recommended by the manufacturer in the owner's manual.

16. Locate a reliable and trustworthy mechanic. The best time to do this is before you need one. Get a recommendation from a friend, relative, or neighbor. A mechanic's reputation follows closely, whether it's good or bad.

17. Increase your automobile insurance deductible. Check with your agent, but chances are excellent that if you increase your deductible to around five hundred dollars, you will receive a greatly reduced premium.

Food

18. Grocery shop with a list. A list is your game plan. Entering the store without it is flirting with financial disaster. The food industry spends some $6 billion a year to weaken your resistance with fancy packaging and compelling displays. Staying out of the store unless absolutely necessary will decrease your exposure time.

19. Arrive at the grocery store with cash only. You will become a much more careful consumer as a cash buyer. This is particularly helpful for the compulsive shopper who would rather stick toothpicks under her fingernails than go through the checkout only to find out she doesn't have enough money.

20. Be brand flexible. Staying loyal to a specific brand might be a noble endeavor, but it will cost you a lot of money in the long run. If you are willing to go with what's on sale and the brand for which you have a doubled coupon, you'll end up keeping more of your money.

21. Shop solo. Your concentration will be better if you leave the kids at home, and you'll get out of the store faster. And your kids won't fall into temptation purposely set by smart marketing organizations. On your next trip to the store, stoop down a bit and check out what's been strategically placed at the eye level of small shopping-cart passengers.

22. Shop at the cheapest store. Most cities have stores with prices that are consistently less. Shop there.

23. Purchase spices from an ethnic food store. Many ethnic markets offer spices in bulk allowing you to purchase as little or as much as you need. Prices? Just a fraction of the prepackaged version.

24. Think vegetarian. Once or twice a week prepare a meatless meal. Serve meat as a side dish or ingredient rather than the entree.

25. Make your own baby food. Experts agree there is no superior nutritional benefit to store-bought baby food compared to food made at home. It only rates high on convenience. Caution: Never substitute your own formula or rice cereal. These are the only exceptions. Use your blender to puree food, then place the food in ice-cube trays and freeze. Food cubes can be stored in zip-type plastic bags and thawed out as needed.

26. Use sale ads. Plan your meals and shopping list around what's on sale this week.

27. Stock up on sale items. If possible, buy enough when it's on sale to last until the next time it hits the sale sheet.

28. Coupons. Use them only for items you'd buy if you didn't have the coupon. Always buy the smallest qualifying size when using a coupon. Join *TheGroceryGame.com* if you are really serious about using coupons to slash your grocery bill.

29. Double coupons. If you are a couponer, try to find a store that doubles their value.

30. Double milk's useful life. Simply add a pinch of salt to milk when first opened. This will retard bacteria growth but will not effect the taste.

31. Investigate store brands. Most grocery-store chains now have their own private labels. In most cases the product is the same as a name brand (usually packaged in the same plant) and labeled under the store's private name. The price is always less. National brands are priced higher because the costs of advertising must be added into the price of the product.

32. Weigh produce. Prepackaged produce must have a minimum weight as printed on the packaging. However, not all potatoes are created equal, so a ten-pound bag may weigh eleven pounds, and a one-pound bag of carrots may weigh more than exactly one pound.

33. Know your prices. Compile your own price book. List all the items you buy regularly, the regular prices from the stores in your area, and the per-unit price (per ounce, for example). Now you will know if a sale is really a sale. Retailers are smart. They know if they put a display at the end of an aisle with a big sign announcing "Special," consumers will assume that it's a bargain. If you know your prices, you won't be fooled.

34. Buy in bulk cautiously. It's no bargain if you end up throwing some away because it spoiled before it could be consumed. Break down large quantities into smaller plastic bags that can be sealed or frozen for future use.

35. Out of sight, out of mind. This can work in your favor or against it. If it's a case of soda pop you picked up at a great price, hiding it under a bed might be a good way to keep the kids from drinking it all in one afternoon. On the other hand, a roast purchased on sale and slipped into the freezer could be forgotten for many months, at which time it might have spoiled. Enzymatic action is not arrested during the freezing period.

36. Buy in season. It takes a little research to know what's coming into season and what's not. Out-of-season produce is the most expensive. Stick to what's plentiful and therefore cheaper.

37. Expired doesn't always mean bad. Because of store policy many foods that are still wholesome are reduced in price when approaching their expiration dates. Many products reduced for quick sale can be a wonderful bargain. Ask the butcher and produce manager what's about to expire. Offer to take it off their hands provided the price is right.

38. Empty the pantry. Most of us have pantries and freezers full of stuff we don't even consider using. By being creative and building menus around what you already have, you might be able to increase the time between grocery-shopping trips. Every day you don't go in the supermarket is another day you can't make an impulsive purchase.

39. Buy local produce. Typically, your local farmer's market will have better prices for far better products. But make a list and stick to it. A beautiful produce market can be as deadly as a beautiful mall. And produce spoils quickly. Buy only what you can reasonably consume.

40. Avoid convenience food. The closer you can stay to basic ingredients such as eggs, sugar, and flour (also known as cooking from scratch!) the less money you will spend.

41. Substitute, experiment. Many people worry about meticulously following the recipe, as if the slightest deviation could change their ambrosia to Alpo. Lighten up. If a recipe calls for a cup of bacon when you have leftover ham in the refrigerator, use the ham.

42. Join a membership warehouse club. Approach this tip with caution. Make sure you will save at least the amount of your membership fee. And get a grip on your impulsive nature or you could end up owning cases of stuff you really cannot use.

43. Eat lunch . . . for dinner. When eating out at dinner time ask to see the lunch menu, or request the luncheon portion of the item you select. Typically you will save 20 percent, with the added benefit of having a lighter meal and not overeating.

Banking costs

44. Don't bounce your account. With banks currently charging around thirty bucks per occurrence, bouncing a check can have quite a punitive result. And don't forget the merchant who took your bad check may have a returned check charge that can be around twenty-five dollars or more. Bouncing checks can be financially deadly.

45. Find a free account. It may take some searching, but there are many banks that offer free accounts with a minimum balance.

46. Ask for free checks. Some banks give free checks, (don't expect anything fancy) if you ask. If you can't manage free checks at least buy your checks directly from a check printer like Checks Unlimited (800-210-0468; *ChecksUnlimited.com*) or Checks in the Mail (800-733-4443; *ChecksInTheMail.com*). You can save up to 60 percent of the price the bank charges.

47. Consider a non-bank. Credit unions are often better and cheaper alternatives for handling your money. Typically, credit unions are smaller, which allows for more personalized service. Credit unions are nonprofit organizations more interested in benefiting their memberships than amassing big profits, which is reflected in lower interest rates and fees, and generally have higher standards when it comes to qualifying borrowers and loan-to-deposit ratios. You need to qualify to join a credit union. Check the Credit Union National Association website at *CUNA.org* to find a credit you can join.

48. Online bill pay. Paying your bills online through your bank's or an independent bill paying site will save you a lot of grief, time and money. You won't have to pay postage and you'll have an electronic record of your banking activity.

49. ATMs. Use only automatic teller machines (ATMs) that are networked into your bank's system and for which you will not be charged a transaction fee.

Utilities

50. Find the water leaks. Give your home this test: Turn off all running water in the house. Find your water meter and take a look. Is it still moving? Chances are you have a water leak and chances are even better it's in your toilet. Put a few drops of food coloring into the toilet's tank. If without flushing the color shows up in the bowl, it's leaking all right! Pick up a simple kit at the home improvement store to fix it yourself.

51. Fix leaky faucets. A faucet leaking sixty drops a minute wastes 113 gallons of water a month. That's 1,356 gallons a year!

52. Use cold water in laundry. The bulk of your laundry is only lightly soiled. Modern-day detergents do just as well with cold as warm. Your colors will last longer too.

53. Experiment. You may be able to use as much as 50 percent less laundry detergent than recommended by the manufacturer, depending on the properties of your water.

54. Install dimmers. Anything you can do to reduce the number of watts you burn will reduce your electricity bill.

55. Select energy-efficient appliances. Use the yellow energy guide labels to make your choices. These appliances consume less energy.

56. Use slow and pressure cookers. Electric burners, gas flames, and traditional ovens are far more expensive to operate than crock pots and pressure cookers. Anything that radiates heat wastes energy.

57. Plug money leaks. Take advantage of your community's free or low-cost programs for insulating your home. Check with your utility companies or community action center.

58. Turn on to efficiency. Install a simple light switch timer in rooms you do not use all the time like the laundry room, basement and so on. Now those lights will go out automatically.

59. Get out of hot water. You'll save heat and water in the dishwasher if you wash only full loads and choose the air-dry option. Don't pre rinse dishes. Lower the water-heater temperature to 120 F. and let the dishwasher do the rest.

60. Create body heat. Raise your body temperature one degree by wearing slacks instead of skirts. Light, long-sleeved sweaters add another two degrees of heat; heavy sweaters, four degrees; and two light sweaters, five degrees (due to the insulation layer of air between them). For extra warmth put on heavy socks with your slippers. Add a quilt to your bed.

61. Turn it down. In the winter keep thermostats set to sixty-five degrees by day and sixty degrees by night unless you are elderly, in poor health, or taking certain types of medication, in which case you should consult your physician.

62. Plug air leaks. Here's how to check for air leaks. Shut the doors and windows. Move a lighted candle around the perimeters of the door or window. If the flame flickers you have an air leak. Plug it with caulk and weather stripping.

63. Install a programmable thermostat. These are reasonably priced and will pay for themselves in no time at all in reduced heating/cooling bills.

64. Turn them off. Turn off electric stove burners and the oven several minutes before specified cooking time. The retained heat will keep on cooking.

65. Multiple dishes. When using the oven, cook several dishes at the same time. Use a timer and don't open the door if at all possible until cooking time is completed.

66. Check refrigerator seal. If it's loose, replace it. Cold air is probably escaping, causing the motor to run more.

67. Write postcards instead of calling. Unless you need to hear a voice, a simple postcard can accomplish the same as a long-distance call. And it's cheap—only twenty-seven cents as of this writing. Keep a stack of postcards by the phone to remind you.

68. Directory assistance. Before calling a company long distance, call 800-555-1212 to see if they have a toll-free number. Most businesses do.

69. Six-second billing. If your present long-distance carrier does not give you six-second billing (instead of billing the next full minute) you may be paying too much. Shop around and find a carrier that does. You could save 8 to 15 percent on your long-distance calling.

70. Free 411. Directory assistance is no longer a free service. You may have a limited number of complimentary calls per month, but after that they are very expensive. Instead, call 800-GOOG411 for businesses, 800-FREE411 for residences. With the latter you'll have to listen to a 10-second commercial while waiting for your number, but hey, it's free.

Entertainment

71. Movie switch. Instead of a movie and dinner, go to a bargained-priced matinee and dinner or dessert after.

72. Have potlucks instead of dinner parties. The ultimate no-obligation gathering where everyone brings a part of the meal is a great social occasion.

73. Escape to the library. You'll be amazed what fun you and your kids can have at the library. You can borrow DVDs, CDs, audio cassettes, and books-on-tape in addition to fabulous books. Some libraries have story time and documentary-film showings.

74. Go for a walk. Chances are you live in a neighborhood you've never explored up close and personally.

75. Write a book of your family's history. Let the kids write and illustrate their own personal chapters.

76. Hold a neighborhood kids' art fair. Display all the artwork and ask adults to purchase their favorites. Let children vote on which charity will receive the proceeds.

77. Be a tourist in your own city. Go online and search your community as if you were a tourist coming for a visit. You will be surprised what activities you will find, many of them free or highly discounted.

Chapter 11

The Least You Need to Know About Fixing, Protecting and Improving Your Credit

"Credit scores are handy for lenders, but they can have enormous repercussions for your wallet, your future, and your peace of mind."
– Liz Pulliam Weston, author, "Your Credit Score"

If just the thought of having to deal with credit reports, credit scores and credit repair a) makes your blood run cold, b) produces heart palpitations, c) causes profuse sweating of the palms, or d) gives you an overwhelming urge to skip this chapter ...

Congratulations! You are normal.

Most of us would prefer just about anything to a face-to-face encounter with our credit reports for any number of reasons, not the least of which may include one—or all—of the following:

Fear. Many women are so afraid to know what's in their credit report they choose denial over reality. I can identify. We figure that as long as we don't know for sure what's in the file, the possibility remains that it's not really *that* bad.

Ignorance. A lot of women simply do not understand credit reports and credit scores—what they are, where they are, who can look at them and why it matters.

Blind faith. There are some who naively trust the supreme credit bureau in the sky to have their best interests at heart. These folks believe that because they pay their bills on time their credit report is automatically a mirror image of such exemplary behavior.

If in the last fifteen years you've applied for any kind of a loan, purchased a cell phone, joined a gym or added basic cable to your lineup of home utilities, you are at least somewhat familiar with the concept of a credit report, also known as a credit file.

Credit reporting agency

To understand your credit report you need to know about credit reporting agencies (CRAs). These are private, for-profit companies that collect credit data and payment records on individuals. They get this information from all kinds of companies that do business such as banks, credit card companies and retail stores. They also comb through public records to find information on everything from bankruptcy filings and court rulings, to judgments, liens and any other kind of legal and financial issue imaginable. They compile the information and sell it to lenders, retailers and other service providers such as insurance companies, phone companies, property management companies and employers, too.

While there are hundreds of CRAs, you need to be concerned with only three: Equifax, Experian and TransUnion. Also known as The Big Three, these CRAs are fierce competitors who are in business to make money.

Businesses like banks, credit card companies, insurance companies, retail stores and so on, subscribe to the services of

CRAs to help them determine if they should give credit to an individual who applies for a credit card, loan or other type of financial obligation. Nearly every application you fill out, whether for credit, to rent an apartment, buy an insurance policy or to get a job has language in it that says if you sign the application, you are giving that company permission to see what is in your credit file. What they find will help them make their decision on whether to deal with you.

With this permission in hand, the company requests your file from the CRA to which it subscribes. Once your deal is completed, each month the company voluntarily reports back to the CRA with specific information on how you are making your payments, how much credit you are using and so on.

The law does not require credit grantors to report information to the CRAs. But the law does require the CRAs to share information that they have. So, theoretically each of your files with the big three should contain identical contents. But do not assume this is the case. It is estimated that about three billion pieces of information are input into credit files every day. While the process is somewhat automated, these companies still rely on humans to disseminate information from credit grantors to CRAs and then into individual files. A tiny slip of a digit could easily land someone else's damaging information in your file.

It is estimated that 70 percent of all individual credit files contain errors. It is imperative that you know what's in each of your files and that you take steps to correct any information that is not true and accurate.

Your credit report

The basic concept of credit reporting is quite simple and based on the premise that past behavior predicts future behavior. A potential lender or other service provider who requires a credit check wants to look at what your past behavior has been when it comes to paying your bills and keeping your word. They believe that past behavior is the best indicator of future behavior. Whether any of this is fair or accurate is a subject for another time. For now you have no choice but to deal with this system.

You are the only person who cares about the accuracy of the contents of your credit files. And you should care deeply because that information, as you are about to learn, shapes your financial future. It determines how much interest you will pay on a mortgage or a credit-card account, the premiums you will pay for insurance. It may also determine if you will be approved to rent an apartment or if you get the job.

If you are of legal age and able to sit up and take nourishment, chances are 100 percent that each CRA has a file with your name on it, which contains more information about you and the way you conduct your financial life than you might dream possible.

The CRAs use the information contained in your credit file to compile a credit report, which is a written document. Each CRA has its own unique style of report, with Experian's generally considered to be the most user-friendly.

There are no limitations on how long a CRA can keep information in your credit file, only on how long they can report negative information. They can, however, continue to report positive information indefinitely. This is why you may see a credit card on your credit report that you got when you were in college and haven't used for many years, but you will not see the fact that you were sixty-days late on a payment because you went on spring break to Daytona Beach and completely forgot to pay your bill.

Negative information doesn't disappear, it only ceases to be reportable on one's credit report after a stipulated period of time.

Credit bureaus are allowed (but not required) by law to report your negative information to potential creditors and others who want to know about you. The result of that can be devastating, all the way from being charged unreasonably high interest rates to losing out on a great apartment or job. While it might feel like those ugly blemishes will remain forever, they cannot. The law provides for specific time limits:

Bankruptcies. Up to ten years from the date of the last activity on the bankruptcy filing.

Past-due accounts, charge-offs, collections, tax liens, judgments and lawsuits from any credit accounts including student loans. Up to seven years from the date of entry, even if the damage is reversed or the account brought current and or paid off.

Inquiries. Up to two years from the date of inquiry. An inquiry is a record of someone checking your credit information. Inquiries come in two categories: "hard inquiries" that occur when a business views your credit report for the purpose of an application and "soft inquiries" that occur when you check your credit file or your current creditors check up on you.

Note: All negative information including bankruptcies, lawsuits, paid tax liens, accounts sent for collection and criminal records may be reported indefinitely when you apply for $150,000 or more of credit or insurance or if you apply for a job with an annual income of at least $75,000.

Your credit score

A credit score is a three-digit number between 300 and 850 that represents how trustworthy you are from the perspective of someone who would lend you money. If you haven't proven yourself trustworthy, your credit score is low; on the other hand, if you repeatedly show yourself trustworthy by paying your bills on time and not overextending yourself with lots of debt, your credit score will be high.

Your credit score is created using a mathematical formula developed by the Fair Isaac & Co., that measures data from your credit report. Credit scores evaluate your payment behavior, debt levels and credit history. Factors like income, race and gender are not measured in the scoring process. Credit scoring systems are used by lenders, insurers, landlords, employers and utility companies to evaluate your credit behavior.

Credit scoring is done by computer software developed by the Fair Isaac & Co., the father of the FICO score. Fair Isaac licenses its highly sophisticated and closely guarded computer scoring model to the CRAs and allows them to develop their own credit score version under a name of their choosing. Fair Isaac has partnered with Equifax to offer its FICO score. If this all sounds confusing, don't worry. Shortly, I'm going to tell you the credit score you need, plus when and how to get it.

More than half of American adults have FICO scores over 700. To be considered "good" you need a FICO score of at least 680. Generally, you need a credit score of at least 720 to get the very best rates on interest, credit, loans, and so on. Your credit score is important because it has such a tremendous effect on your financial life.

Who determines a credit score?

While a lot of what goes into determining one's credit score remains a trade secret of the Fair Isaac & Co., they have revealed the five main elements that go into scoring one's credit and the weight each carries in determining that final score for credit reporting in the United States:

Payment history 35 percent. Making on-time payments is important. To get some perspective, 6 out of 10 Americans don't have a single late payment on their credit reports.

How much you owe 30 percent. The score looks at the total amount your owe at any given moment compared to how much you could owe if you maxed out all of your credit limits. These two amount should not even be close. The bigger the gap between your balance and your limit, the better.

Length of credit history 15 percent. Your credit score likes long history and considers the age of your oldest account and the average age of all your accounts.

New credit 10 percent. Your credit score doesn't like to see new applications for credit. To give you some perspective, the average American has not opened an account for 20 months.

Types of credit used 10 percent. Your credit score likes a "healthy mix" of credit, whatever that means. No one is completely sure because this is part of the puzzle that Fair Isaac & Co. keeps vague. However, to get the highest score you need to show a mix of credit in your history—like a mortgage, an automobile loan, and so on—not only credit cards.

How to improve your score

The best things you can do to improve your credit score:

- ✤ Pay down your debts.

- ✤ Do not open new credit card accounts.

- ✤ Pay all of your bills on time.

If you follow these three rules, your credit score will take care of itself over time. Don't worry about it; instead, concentrate on what's on your credit report. Remember that your score is all of the information on your credit report boiled down to three digits.

How to repair your credit

Correct errors in your credit file. This requires a frequent review of your credit report. Look for mistakes in everything from the spelling of your name to your address and similar personal information. Next make sure that all of the information reported is true and accurate.

You cannot remove negative information just because you don't like it or because the negatives are no longer active (for example you may have completely paid an account that was once 60-days late), but you can dispute non-factual information and outright errors. Your credit report will come with instructions for how to dispute items on the report. Do not hesitate to dispute old negatives and others that you cannot verify to be factually correct.

Use credit infrequently. In fact, stop using your credit cards at all. This will increase that gap between your limits and your outstanding balances.

If you must, use the oldest card. Remember your credit file likes a nice long history. If you have to use a card, use the one you've had the longest to make sure this history is being re-ported and considered in your credit score.

One last word on credit repair: Do not hire a company to re-pair your credit. First, they cannot do anything legally that you cannot do for yourself. But most importantly, the FTC warns that most of the companies are scam artists. They collect a huge fee from you up front, then disappear into the night—with your personal and private information.

Get your credit report

You can get your credit report for free, no questions asked, at *AnnualCreditReport.com.* This is a service required by the Fed-eral Trade Commission that allows you one free download of your credit report each year from each of The Big Three CRAs, Equifax, Experian, and TransUnion. Since most of the time the three reports are substantially the same, you can get your credit report for free every four months.

Do not use any other service to get your report or you will end up being forced to sign up for services and pay fees that you don't have to pay.

Even if the word FREE is plastered all over the ads and web-sites (and I include Experian, Equifax and TransUnion here be-cause they want to get you to pay for the information they have on you), do not fall for it. Let me repeat this: The only place you can get your credit reports for free is *AnnualCreditReport.com*, or call 877-322-8228.

The worst offender of the free report that is anything but free is the heavily advertised *FreeCreditReport.com.* Don't go near this company!

Once you have your report, read it very carefully to make sure it's accurate. If you find something that isn't, start disputing. You'll find out how to do that in the information you will receive with your credit report. False information on your credit report does nothing but hurt you, and you should seek to have it re-moved from your report as soon as possible.

Get your credit score

There are different methods of calculating credit scores. FICO, developed by Fair Isaac & Co., is used by many mortgage lenders that use a risk-based system to determine the possibility that the borrower may default on financial obligations to the mortgage lender.

The credit bureaus all use the FICO model and software, but use it to create their own version of credit scores. Put it this way: Your credit score comes in three flavors: TransUnion offers its Beacon Score, Experian calls its version Plus Score, and Equifax has partnered with Fair Isaac to offer the FICO score. Each score, while supposedly based on the same information in your credit report, will be slightly different because each has its unique scoring scale.

Despite anything you hear or read to the contrary, there is no way that you can get your credit score for free. You will pay a fee. The question is how much you will pay. Those who advertise your credit score for free will require you to sign up for a very expensive annual contract.

My recommendation is this: If you plan to apply for a mortgage or car loan within the next six months, it is helpful for you to know your score ahead of time. In this case, get your FICO score from *MyFico.com*. The cost is about $15.95 for the standard score. Caution: You will be pressured to sign up for more expensive plans and monitoring services. You do not need these. Just your plain vanilla credit score will do.

There is an alternative to paying for your credit score: Estimate what it is based on what you find in your credit report from *AnnualCreditReport.com*, using the FICO Score Estimator at *MyFico.com/ficocreditscoreestimator*. Unless you have a specific need, estimating your score may be good enough for now. And it is a free alternative to paying for your score.

Opt out

Under the Fair Credit Reporting Act (FCRA), CRAs are permitted to include your name on lists used by creditors or insurers to make firm offers of credit or insurance that are not initiated by you. Sometimes these "firm offers" show up as pre-approved offers in your mailbox from credit card companies and others.

The FCRA also provides you the right to "opt out," which prevents CRAs from providing your credit file information for marketing purposes.

My advice is that you should opt out for yourself and for everyone in your household. You can do this online at *OptOut Prescreen.com* or by calling 888-567-8688. You will be required to give your social security number but do not worry about this. They have it already.

I have always found this matter of credit gathering, analyzing and scoring to be a little creepy. I mean, who among us would be comfortable having some private industry analyze and score anything else about our personal lives—without our knowledge? Like the way we dress or how we keep house. See what I mean? Creepy.

But the truth is that the consumer credit industry is here to stay and it's bigger than all of us. We have no say in whether the CRAs set up files with our names and Social Security numbers on them. We cannot tell our creditors to stop dealing with these agencies, nor can we stop them from creating credit scores based on how we behave with our money.

Sometimes we've just got to play along to get along. And when it comes to credit files and credit scores, that is the responsible thing that we must do.

Chapter 12

The Least You Need to Know About Preparing for Emergencies

"You lazy people can learn by watching an anthill. Ants don't have leaders, but they store up food during harvest season. How long will you lie there doing nothing at all?"
– Proverbs 6:6-9

No matter your situation—even if you are up to your eyeballs in credit-card debt—you must have an emergency fund, which at Debt-Proof Living we call a Contingency Fund. Every household needs one. It is as essential to you getting out of debt as water is to your health. Without it you won't go far.

Creating your Contingency Fund

In chapter 7 you learned the second most important thing you must do with your money: Save at least 10 percent in a savings account. Now let's give that account a name—Contingency

Fund—and a savings goal: At least enough money to pay all of your bills for at least three months; six is better. Or, in the interest of simplicity, let's set your goal at $10,000.

I'm sure that since you're still with me here, you're at least considering the value of establishing this kind of emergency fund. First, face the facts regarding job and income security. Don't count on it. With technology increasing at a breakneck speed and the nation's economic system having more peaks and valleys than a roller coaster, it's almost certain that sometime your income will at least temporarily be cut off. It's going to happen, so plan on it instead of being blindsided by it.

Start with baby steps. I agree that a figure equal to six months' income is rather overwhelming—paralyzingly so. Instead of focusing on that big number, cut it up into bite-sized pieces. How much would it take for you to live one week without income? Let's just assume that number is something like six hundred dollars. Now I'm not saying that would cover your house payment or rent, but six hundred dollars might be enough to keep gas in the car, food on the table, and the utilities paid.

Focus on saving enough money so that your Contingency Fund (CF) equals one week's living expenses. That is an achievable goal. Then move to two weeks, a month and so on. In no time, if you keep your eye on the goal, you will achieve a fully funded Contingency Fund. And that is going to make all the difference in the world for you. Your sense of financial fear will disappear. You will find yourself less prone to overspend. Your financial confidence will soar!

The source for building your CF is the 10 percent you are saving from every paycheck (remember chapter 7). This is more important to your financial confidence than you will ever know.

It's counterintuitive

I know this may be grating on your nerves—the idea that you should be saving money. I agree that when you're in debt and so anxious to get out of debt, it doesn't make sense to keep money for yourself. Common sense says you should be sending your creditors every nickel you can scrape together.

It *seems* right perhaps, but it's not. That's the same "common sense" that said it's okay to use credit cards to buy stuff and pay for it later; the same "common sense" that says if you are severely overweight you should not eat again until you have achieved your goal weight. It's a nice thought, but it's just not going to happen. You'll be able to follow that kind of thinking only until you get hungry if we're talking weight, or until something unexpected happens when talking about money and credit.

How it grows

Under the debt-proof living plan, 10 percent of your net paycheck goes straight into your CF before you pay any bills.

Five reasons

Face it. Getting out of debt is no simple feat. It takes commitment, knowledge and most of all endurance. You didn't get into this much debt overnight, so it's going to take longer than a few days to get out. This will not be a sprint, but rather a marathon. Your CF will be the assurance you need to see it to the finish line.

1. It is the antidote for your credit-card habit. Just knowing you have money in the bank quiets that thing inside of you that demands to have stuff right now, even when you have no money to pay for it.

2. It counteracts that pathetic feeling of being broke. One of the reasons you are in debt is that you can't stand that feeling of being poor.

No one likes being broke, but some of us like it a lot less than others. Curiously, a pocket of credit cards makes us feel rich in a really false way. Knowing you have money in the bank is the authentic way to not feel broke—even when you are determined to not touch the money you have stashed away.

3. It gives you an alternative to hitting the panic button. When you're broke, you live on the edge of panic. And when even the smallest thing happens, even if it is not a true emergency, it feels like one because you press the panic button. Having money in the bank allows you to calm down so you can think reasonably.

4. It's the lifesaver that keeps you afloat while going through deep waters. If you can make it all the way from right now to paying off your last debt without facing some unexpected expense (tires, water heater, medical expense, car repair, and so on), you will be fortunate indeed. And you'll arrive with an intact CF.

The chances are far greater, however, that while on your journey to becoming debt-free something unexpected will happen. It's your CF that will allow you to keep going without having to run back to your credit cards for a bailout. Just imagine how defeated you will feel should that happen. Of course you can start again, but you want to do everything possible to avoid getting off course.

5. It's your guarantee that you'll make it to the finish line. I say this on the basis of my own experience and that of countless readers who are now debt-free—having a CF, whether fully funded or in process, is the secret to your debt-free success. It's that second wind we all depend on when we've come to the end of our endurance, but there's still more journey ahead.

Your CF will keep you going and going. And going some more until you pay off that last dollar of debt.

A Contingency Fund creates the margin you need to move away from the edge. Since my financial reformation I have come to look upon this matter of an emergency fund as wise advice. More than that, I believe it is absolutely essential if financial peace is to be achieved, and I've learned it is possible to make this seeming impossibility become reality.

For some of us "emergency" can mean anything from the midyear sale at Nordstrom to a 3:13 A.M. hospital trip. I used to operate much like the federal government. Once a situation was worthy of being declared an emergency, all limitations on spending were overridden.

Christmas became an emergency. Perhaps you've experienced it: It's December 15, the kids are entitled to a great Christmas, which is measured, of course, by the number and size of gifts. We have no money. We call the credit card companies to plead for credit-line increases. Given the increases, we now feel authorized to run wild, to purchase stuff that will be forgotten before the bills arrive in January.

You probably know of someone, perhaps yourself, who has been in some way separated from their income. It can be due to a job layoff, a tragic disability, or any number of other reasons. The loss of one's income can be one of life's most devastating events.

Two cases in point

Tom and Lisa

The Moores live paycheck to paycheck on Tom's salary. There's never enough money. They're habitually late with their bills but manage somehow to get caught up several times a year. Tom is able to work overtime during tax season, which helps a lot. However, due to downsizing at his firm, Tom is given a two-week notice of his scheduled layoff. Like a batter who's been "dusted" by an opposing pitcher, Tom and Lisa are knocked to the ground emotionally. What will they do? They're one month behind on the mortgage payment, both of their new cars are leased, and Lisa's made reservations for herself and the girls to fly to Florida next week to visit her parents.

They have no sources from which to draw. Tom hasn't been with the firm long enough to warrant severance pay. Their credit cards are maxed out, as is the equity in the house.

Lisa recalls that a preapproved line of credit from a big finance company came in the mail a few days ago. She madly rummages through the trash, finds it, and breathes a sigh of relief. At least they have $3,500. She decides not to bother Tom with the matter because the last thing he needs to worry about is more debt.

Tom spends the next two weeks putting together his resume and sends out hundreds of copies with no particular rhyme or reason.

After eight incredibly long weeks, Tom finally gets his first unemployment check, but it doesn't begin to cover the stacks of bills growing on the table. Lisa is beside herself with worry, wishes she'd never gone to Florida, has gone through the $3,500 from the finance company, and is about to lose her mind because Tom spends every day pacing and stewing.

The first foreclosure notice arrives three months following Tom's layoff. Creditors call daily. Lisa's stomach is in a knot most of the time. She has one nerve remaining, and it's about shot.

Finally, after four incomeless months, Tom receives a job offer. It's not exactly what he'd hoped for and the pay cut will be hard to handle, but it's a job with a paycheck. He jumps at the offer and within two weeks receives his first, albeit smaller, paycheck.

It's been two years since Tom's job change. He's not that happy in this position but has decided to grin and bear it. Lisa has taken a part-time job at the kids' school and hates every minute of it. They've still not recovered from the devastation of the layoff. Their debts are higher than ever, and their credit report is all but ruined. Worst of all, they're no more prepared for a future layoff than they were before.

Greg and Jody

The Spencers have three children. Jody has a small desktop-publishing business in their home, and Greg is a foreman at the local steel plant. Greg participates faithfully in his company's 401(k) plan, contributing 5 percent of his gross pay into the fund, and the company matches his contributions. He's been doing this for years since he started at the plant during high school. In addition, another 10 percent is deducted and automatically deposited to their online savings account (OSA) that's been earning from 3 to 5 percent interest. Greg has been at the plant long enough to know that good times come and go. While the chances are fairly slim, he could be laid off. Even if it was temporary, he needs to know they have money set aside to cover the bills.

As a result of deep cuts in defense spending, Greg's company loses the government contract they had for many years. In no time at all, pink slips are distributed; and as you might have guessed, Greg receives his. While of course this is not good news, it is not devastating.

Greg spends the next two weeks dreaming and exploring options. He and Jody talk about all the things they've wished they could pursue but have rejected because of Greg's job.

They withdraw just the minimum amount needed from their OSA to cover their basic living necessities during the time between Greg's last paycheck and first unemployment check. They also supplement the unemployment checks with their emergency funds to keep the bills paid and food on the table.

Greg puts together a résumé based on his dream of becoming a professional photographer. He includes information on competitions he's won as well as examples of his work. Over the following two months, he follows up every possible lead in the area of photography and lands not one, but two interviews.

Greg is offered a position as an apprentice with the largest commercial photography company in the city, and he eagerly accepts. The pay is quite similar to what he's been making at the plant, but it lacks the fringe benefits.

During the first year of Greg's new job, he and Jody are determined to reduce expenses sufficiently to allow for replacement of the money they took from their emergency fund. They increase the semimonthly contribution to 15 percent instead of 10 so as to repay it more quickly.

Greg and Jody did not have a negative reaction to their set of circumstances. In fact, Greg looks back upon the layoff as one of the best things that ever happened to him. This blessing disguised as a pink slip opened the doors for him to blend his life's work with his creative passions. They didn't miss a beat in paying their house payment and utility bills. Because they had the peace of mind an emergency fund can bring, they actually had fun during this unexpected time off between jobs.

Tom and Lisa, on the other hand, suffered greatly. Their relationship was dealt a blow because Lisa activated that $3,500 loan without Tom knowing. Tom became so depressed Lisa didn't even want to be around him. The girls became needlessly fearful that they would be homeless. And each month rather than getting ahead they fell further and further behind as their debt grew and grew.

Tom is anything but fond of his job, but he feels hopelessly stuck. Lisa resents having to work, and it now looks as if she will need to find a full-time job in the fall. Tom's layoff has greatly altered their lives, and they are much worse off for it.

Irregular, intermittent and unpredictable expenses

Expenses that don't occur on a regular monthly basis are often forgotten. When they rise up to remind us of their existence we often refer to them as emergencies. They're also considered financial crises.

Irregular, intermittent, or unpredictable expenses would include things like insurance premiums, new brakes on the car, veterinarian bills, vacations, clothes, and Christmas, to name a few. They are expenses that don't occur at precisely the same time or the same amount every month, month after month.

My theory is this: Most of us have found a way to handle mortgage or rent payments, grocery bills, utilities, car payments—our monthly expenses. It's all the other things that creep up on us and scare us to death that send us running to the credit cards or some other form of credit. If we could just come up with a way to predict those expenses, we could plan ahead and never be caught off-guard again.

A management tool I have created for my *Debt-Proof Living*

family is something called a Freedom Account. It is perfectly designed for being prepared for irregular, unpredictable, or intermittent expenses rather than being derailed by them.

Here are the basic guidelines for creating your own Freedom Account:

1. Using a year's worth of check registers, credit-card statements, and paid receipts, reconstruct the irregular, intermittent, or unpredictable expenses you had to deal with last year. These are things like medical and dental expenses, taxes, insurance, vacations, and Christmas.

2. Annualize these figures (multiply so that you come up with a dollar figure for the year) and divide each by twelve. One-twelfth of each expense is what you need to set aside each month in anticipation of these expenses.

3. Open a separate checking account to handle your Freedom Account.

4. Each month deposit one-twelfth payment for each of the above items.

5. Set up a notebook with a separate page for each category or subaccount. Each month enter that month's deposit and calculate a new balance.

6. As irregular, unpredictable, or intermittent expenses come up for which you have set up a subaccount, write out a check from the Freedom Account to make the payment. Record it on the subaccount page as a debit, and calculate the new balance.

Members of *Debt-Proof Living Online* enjoy a very powerful tool—the Freedom Account Manager. Here's how it works: You set up your Freedom Account checking account at your bank or credit union of choice. Then you set up your Freedom Account Manager at *DebtProofLiving.com*, where all of your information is passcoded and very secure. You can see at a glance exactly how much you have available in each subaccount, keep track of all your Freedom Account deposits and transfer money from one subaccount to another, right online at our secure site.

Used properly, your Freedom Account will revolutionize your

finances. Being prepared for emergencies, large or small, is great all on its own, to say nothing of all the fringe benefits like less stress, more financial options and an overall feeling of maturity, responsibility and well-being.

Chapter 13

The Least You Need to Know about Your Financial Condition

"Whoever is faithful in small matters will be faithful in large ones; whoever is dishonest in small matters will be dishonest in large ones. If, then, you have not been faithful in handling worldly wealth, how can you be trusted with true wealth?"
– Luke 16:10-11

Becoming a mother to two babies born in quick succession was for me just short of completely overwhelming. All the feeding, cleaning, changing, burping, sleeping, nurturing, cuddling—it's hard to know if you're doing things right and the baby is developing correctly. We relied heavily on the weighing, measuring, assessing and testing to tell us how we were doing with the growth and development.

Most of our well-baby evaluations revealed that we were on track and making good progress. And when the results were not as glowing, we were grateful for early detection because that allowed for swift intervention. I can tell you we would have been in big trouble had we waited many years to have our boys' growth and development assessed.

Caring for your financial situation is quite similar to raising children. You do what you think is the right thing on a day-by-day basis, but without that regular weighing, measuring, assessing and evaluating you don't know if you are on the right track or not. Thankfully you don't have to haul yourself into the office of a professional financial assessor. You can learn to do all of the "weighing and measuring" yourself to assess your personal financial situation.

It doesn't matter if you're single or married, if you handle the finances in your home or not—every woman needs to possess certain basic financial skills that enable her to balance a checkbook and develop a Spending Plan, Net Worth Statement and Cash Flow Statement.

Balance your checkbook

I can nearly hear a muffled moaning sound of "Why do I have to do this?!" Look, I of all people know this can be a rash-inducing assignment, but once you understand the process it is so simple you'll be surprised that you ever avoided balancing your checkbook.

As for the "why," you need to do this because you cannot trust your bank or credit union to be perfect. And you cannot trust yourself to never forget to record an ATM or debit-card transaction. Banks make mistakes and you should assume that they do this often. Another reason: If you make a mistake or forget to post an ATM withdrawal, debit-card purchase, or other transaction in your checkbook register, you may start bouncing checks and incurring horrible penalty fees.

If you use personal finance software like Quicken, Money or Mvelopes to manage your bank account, you may assume that you do not need to balance your account, thinking the software will do this for you. That is a wrong assumption. You still must reconcile at least once each month. The software just makes it a bit easier.

Okay, let's get started.

To me, the hardest thing about a checking account is remembering to write down the amount of a check as it is written. We found duplicate checks to be the solution. Each check has its own carbon copy record that remains in the wallet once you've pulled out the check. With this contemporaneous record, you will always know to whom and for how much you wrote each check.

Before you even start this reconciling procedure, make sure you have calculated a current balance in your checkbook that reflects all the checks you've written and the deposits you've made since the last time your account was reconciled.

To balance your checkbook assemble the following:

1. Your checking-account statement that comes monthly from the bank.

2. Canceled checks. Not many banks (any?) enclose the actual checks any longer. But you may get photocopies.

3. Your checkbook register. ATM receipts, debit-card transaction receipts and paycheck stubs.

4. Checkbook Balancing Worksheet (it's on page 151).

5. Pencil and eraser.

6. Calculator.

Step 1. Sort deposit slips and checks into two groups. Divide automatic teller machine slips into deposits (put with deposit slips) and cash withdrawal slips, transfers, and payments (put with checks).

Step 2. Look at the statement and compare the actual canceled check with the amount of the check as noted on the statement. Banks do make errors now and again. For instance, you might have written a check for $48.26 but the check shows up on your statement as $84.26. Circle or make note of any discrepancies.

Step 3. Go through your check stubs or register and check off each check that has been enclosed with this statement. If you have a stub or entry in your register for which you do not have the paid check in the statement, list that amount under "checks outstanding."

Step 4. Look on the statement for any bank charges, such as the cost of checks, service fees, or overdraft fees. Enter these bank charges in your check register and deduct the amount just as you would if you'd written a check for this amount.

Step 5. Look on the statement for automatic or direct withdrawals you may have authorized, such as insurance payments or investment transfers. Make sure these are deducted in your register just as if you'd written a check for that amount.

Step 6. Look for direct deposits (some people have their paychecks, dividends, or social security checks deposited directly, and some checking accounts earn interest). Make sure each has been entered into your check registry as a credit and added to the balance.

Step 7. Make sure you have entered every ATM withdrawal and debit-card transaction into your checkbook and your statement doesn't have a few extra on there that might belong to someone else. It could happen, you know.

Okay, now that you've gotten everything together and your checkbook is current, you're ready to move on to the Checkbook Balancing Worksheet.

Most bank statements have a worksheet printed on the back. I can nearly guarantee it won't be as easy to read and user-friendly as mine, but feel free to proceed with your worksheet of choice. Just fill in the blanks.

I'm going to assume you balanced to the penny the first time out. Let me be the first to offer my congratulations. Look, I of all people know what a major accomplishment this is. Feels good, doesn't it?

Now, in the off-chance your checkbook balance and bank-statement balance are not exactly the same, don't panic. Just find the error. Here are some suggestions for finding it quickly.

Checkbook Balancing Worksheet

My balance according
to the Bank

My balance according
to my checkbook

These two balances should agree.

Outstanding Checks
(Checks, debit card purchases and ATM
withdrawals that do not appear on my
bank statement.)

Date	Chk #	Amt
Total:		

Outstanding Deposits
(Deposits I made but do not appear on
my bank statement)

Date	Amt
Total:	

Ending balance on
bank statement

+ Plus outstanding
deposits

= Equals
Subtotal

– Minus outstanding
checks

=

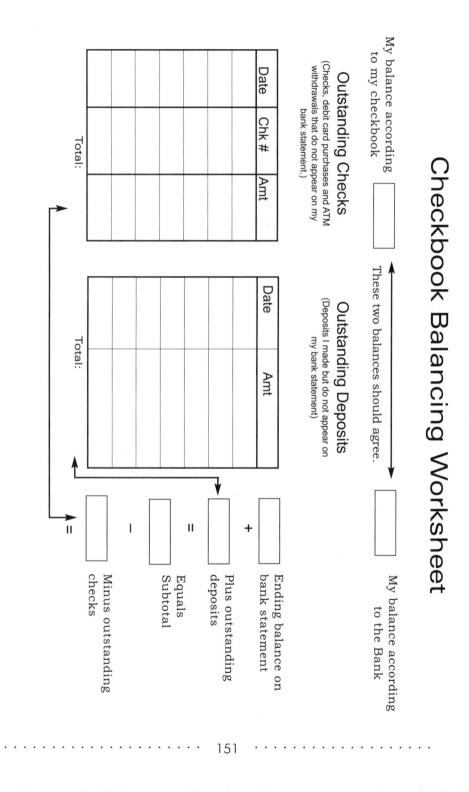

Is there an error in your addition or subtraction?

Did you deduct all the bank charges from your checkbook balance before you started on the worksheet?

Does the amount you're "out of balance" ring a bell? Does it just happen to be the exact amount of that cash withdrawal you took last week and forgot to write down?

Divide the out-of-balance amount by nine. If the answer is a whole number (nothing behind the decimal point) there's a very good chance you have transposed a figure. Example: The check was for $8.59 but you wrote down $8.95 in your checkbook.

Did you fail to write down a deposit? (Happy find!)

If you just can't find the error, your bank will be more than happy to. Take your statement, checkbook, and worksheet to the bank with you. Leaving the mystery unsolved will only set you up for a bigger problem next month. You're going to be in a pickle if you let this go too long.

How to Develop a Spending Plan

When we were children we were accountable to grownups for just about everything, from making our beds to completing homework. As we matured, little by little that accountability shifted. By the time we left home, we were no longer accountable to our parents and other authority figures; we were accountable to ourselves. Well, that's the way it's supposed to work. But the process must have a high breakdown rate because too many of us end up accountable to no one for our personal finances.

Let's see how accountable you've been to yourself with your finances. How much did you spend on food last month? Auto repairs? credit card payments? Late fees? Cab fare? Haven't a clue or even a vague notion? Well, don't feel too badly. Most people have a difficult time coming up with anything close to exact figures for such routine expenses.

I suppose denial has something to do with it. If you have no idea what your bank balance is, it's easier to fool yourself, by adding a digit or two to the amount you think might be in there, than to face the reality of not having enough to buy a newspaper, let alone cover the cash withdrawal you pulled out of the automatic teller machine last night.

Assuming you are sick and tired of living in a financial fog, then you should welcome the bright light that only a precise spending record will turn on in your life. I wouldn't be surprised if such clarity might be a bit intimidating. The truth is not often welcome, especially if it points out problem areas in our lives. You may be hesitant to bring into sharp focus the exact nature of your finances. Whatever your fears, please do not underestimate the value and importance of recording your spending. Knowing the truth really will set you free.

Daily spending record

The first step in developing a Spending Plan is to keep a daily spending record for thirty days, or one month. This is simply a written account of money spent during a specific day. Writing it down is the only way to find out where all the money goes. If you are part of a team where one person handles the bulk of the money, this is going to require a bit of teamwork. If you have an uncooperative partner, start by becoming accountable to yourself for whatever amount of money you control. As you become more adept at managing those funds—who knows?—you might end up controlling much more; so don't underestimate the importance of adopting this invaluable new behavior.

From now on you will look at each month as having four weeks, regardless of what day of the week the first falls on or how many total days are in the month: Days 1-7 will always be Week 1; Days 8-14 will always be Week 2; Days 15-21, Week 3; Days 22–End of Month, Week 4. It doesn't matter that the fourth week of every month will have anywhere from six to nine days.

Get yourself a little notebook or small pad of paper. Each day start with a fresh page and put the current date at the top. Each time you spend cash, make a credit card purchase (yes, write it down because you've spent the money even if it doesn't feel that way), or write a check, jot down two entries: what and how much. Don't neglect writing checks into the check register, too,

Daily Spending Records

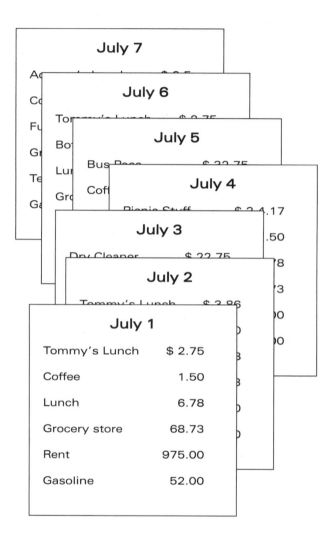

July 7

Ac
Co
Fu
Gi
Te
Ga

July 6

Tommy's Lunch $ 2.75
Bo
Lui
Gr

July 5

Bus Pass $ 22.75
Cof

July 4

Picnic Stuff $ 24.17
.50
8
3
)0
)0

July 3

Dry Cleaner $ 22.75

July 2

Tommy's Lunch $ 2.86

July 1

Tommy's Lunch	$ 2.75
Coffee	1.50
Lunch	6.78
Grocery store	68.73
Rent	975.00
Gasoline	52.00

since this spending record is not taking the place of your regular financial recordkeeping.

That's it. One page per day, every day. No time off. No endless details and no totals (for now). Given the miracle of twenty-one, this should become a habit in about three weeks.

In the case of a partnership, both you and your spouse should keep a daily spending record, even if one spouse handles very little of the family income. Remember, this is not an exercise in spying on each other or making sure neither partner has any money to call their own, but simply an effort to determine where the money goes. This may not need to be a long-term activity (for some it becomes a lifelong habit), but it is certainly necessary for at least ninety days in order to develop a spending plan.

A daily spending record has a very specific purpose—to gather the information necessary to formulate a weekly spending record. Four weekly records will help you produce your first full monthly spending record.

It's the fringe benefits of this activity that are going to surprise you. If you are true to yourself and diligently write down every dollar, dime, even every penny, you spend, your spending activities are going to change dramatically simply because of this commitment to record. I don't know why. Perhaps it makes us stop spending unconsciously. Knowing you'll have to write it down makes you think twice before you drop a twenty-dollar bill on something you might otherwise have purchased in a moment of impulsiveness.

Expense categories

You have fixed expenses (car payment, rent, mortgage payment, etc.) and flexible expenses (food, gasoline, utilities, etc.). You need to come up with a list of expenses that are unique to you and your family. Try to be neither too detailed nor too general. Too many categories will be unmanageable. Too few will give you only a vague idea of where you are. The average family will likely have fifteen to twenty categories. Looking through your checkbook register or your canceled checks will help you recall expenses you have on a recurring basis.

Weekly spending record

A weekly spending record is going to bring further clarity because it will summarize your daily spending activities. At the end of Week 1, gather the seven days' spending records (if you are a partnership, ideally you'll have fourteen of these; if single, just seven). Using this information, make up a simple weekly spending record similar to the illustration on the following page. This is as simple a listing as the daily records, except that it has a total amount spent for the week.

Average monthly income

Regardless of your payroll schedule or the frequency with which you receive other sources of income, next you need to come up with your average monthly income, that number which when multiplied by twelve equals your annual gross income. Note: I prefer to work with a gross figure (before any taxes or other withholding is applied), however you may be more comfortable working with a net figure, or your actual take-home pay. You decide. Just be consistent once you've made the decision. If working with gross, be sure to include expense categories for each of those items for which money is withheld from your wages.

Here is a simple formula for determining your average monthly income. If you are paid ...

Weekly: Multiply your income by 4.333

Biweekly: Multiply your income by 2.167

Semimonthly: Multiply your income by 2

Quarterly: Divide your income by 3

Annually: Divide your income by 12

When determining your average monthly income, include all sources such as salary, wages, commission, dividend and interest income, child-support payments, alimony, etc. If you get it on a regular basis, can predict its arrival, and can spend it, it's income.

Weekly Spending Record

Month of January
Week # 1 (Days 1-7)

Savings	$100.00
Giving	100.00
Rent	950.00
Groceries	183.57
Food (away from home)	52.73
Telephone	68.74
Gasoline	40.00
Auto oil change	29.95
Clothing	53.87
Property taxes	200.00
School tuition	76.00
Publications	16.45
Gifts (Grandma's Birthday)	19.58
Home Depot (household maint.)	58.68
Medical	24.25
Children's school supplies	15.86
Credit card payment	158.00
Other debt payment	75.00
Total	**$2,222.68**

Sample Monthly Spending Record

Category	Wk 1	Wk 2	Wk 3	Wk 4	Total
Savings	$100.00	$100.00	$100.00	$100.00	$400.00
Giving	100.00	100.00	100.00	100.00	400.00
Rent	950.00				950.00
Groceries	183.57	237.65	58.00	74.34	553.56
Food (away)	52.73	14.50	5.76	45.85	118.84
Electricity		87.50			87.50
Heating Fuel					-------
Telephone	68.74				68.74
Car payments			279.00	183.00	462.00
Gasoline	40.00	40.00	40.00	40.00	160.00
Auto maint.	29.95		37.50		67.45
Insurance		72.50		22.00	94.50
Clothing	53.87	89.00		12.98	155.85
Property taxes	200.00				200.00
School tuition	76.00				76.00
Publications	16.45				16.45
Gifts	19.58				19.58
Entertainment		25.00		10.50	35.50
Haircuts				17.50	17.50
House Maint.	58.68	21.53	15.67		95.88
Medical	24.25				24.25
Children's Misc	15,86		24.00	10.00	49.86
Credit cards	158.00				158.00
Other debt	75.00				75.00
Miscellaneous					-------
Totals	$2,222.68	787.68	659.93	616.17	$4,286.46

Monthly Spending Plan						
Category	Wk 1	Wk 2	Wk 3	Wk 4	Total Spent	Plan to spend

_____ Average Monthly Income

_____ Less Total Actually Spent This Month

_____ Amount Underspent or <Overspent>

Monthly Spending Record

Once you have completed daily and weekly spending records for an entire month, you should transfer this information to a monthly spending record. Now the truth is coming into clear focus. Once you have totaled your entire month's spending activities, fill in your average monthly income and deduct your expenses. If you have a negative number, you must have used the credit cards quite a few times this month. This will show you how much you are overspending or underspending your income.

Keep in mind, this month will not be duplicated every month, because of irregular, intermittent, and unpredictable expenses. Repeating this process for the next two months will give you an even clearer picture.

Monthly Spending Plan

If you are diligent and continue recording your spending, developing weekly and monthly spending records, something remarkable is bound to happen. You are going to automatically see where your problem with spending lies.

I once received a letter from a lady who shared her astonishment that given her current level of spending she would spend well over $1,500 on cappuccino in the coming year. Once she started writing down her daily expenditures, it was clear that at three dollars a cup and sometimes more than once a day, this little treat was quickly destroying her solvency. She saw the big picture, determined that there were other things she'd much rather do with $1,500 each year, and made the decision on her own to make some changes. A budget would not have pointed out her problem. That's the difference between a budget and a plan. I much prefer any term that does not include the word *budget*.

Back to our monthly spending plan. The difference between the monthly spending record and the monthly spending plan is one little column, "Plan to Spend Next Month." Based on what was spent in the previous month, what do you need to spend next month to make sure your expenses are less than your average monthly income? You decide. This is your spending plan; it's your life.

Can you get that fast-food amount down a few notches by cooking at home? Anything you can do to cut that huge heating bill in half? (Yes, there are lots of things you can do.) And that entertainment category. Yikes! Is this really where you want that much money to go each month?

If your situation is severe—cutting out all optionals leaves you still spending more than you earn—you may need to look at some drastic cost-cutting measures, such as like moving into less expensive housing or selling a car. There are only three ways to change this picture: increase income, decrease expenses, or sell assets.

And so you plan for the coming month. On the form for the next month, you fill in the "Plan to Spend" column ahead of time. As the weeks unfold and you fill in the actual spending, all kinds of lights are going to come on. You'll start projecting what will happen at the end of the month if you keep spending the way you did in month one. This is called managing your money, and in time it's going to feel really good. This is how to start taking control of your money instead of letting it control you.

Your Personal Economy

You'd have to be living under a rock somewhere to not be aware that the national economy goes through cycles of growth and decline. And people get all nervous when a recession is predicted and the economy is declared to be slowing down. And that's pretty much wasted energy.

Forget the national economy for now. Instead focus on your *personal economy*. It is not a foregone conclusion that your personal economy will reflect the national economy's ups and down.

In fact, plenty of people see their economic well-being decline while the rest of the country is doing great, while others make great financial progress when the rest of the nation is facing a major downturn. When you're secure in a good job it doesn't matter to you if the the national unemployment rate is a low

4 percent or creating gloomy headers at 5 percent. But everything changes when you are unemployed. It won't matter if the national rate is high or low, because when you're the one with the pink slip all of a sudden the real unemployment rate has just reached 100 percent.

As difficult as it may be to face the truth of where you are financially, it's the right thing to do. After all, you'll never figure out how to get where you want to be until you know where you are.

There are three important personal economic indicators that generally reveal your overall financial condition and predict your financial future—your gross household income, your cash flow and your net worth.

Gross income

This is the total of the income of all household wage earners before taxes, retirement contributions and other expenses that are deducted from your paycheck(s), together with any other sources of income like dividends and interest. The easiest way to come up with this number is to look at your most current pay stubs and other statements that show any and all income. Once you have your current gross annual income (or you can use a monthly figure if your income is fairly stable), compare this number to your gross household income in the same period one year ago.

If you are making at least 2 percent more than you were one year ago, you are just about keeping up with inflation. Your money is losing value through inflation because it takes at least 2 percent more each year to purchase the same goods and services as before.

If your gross income has increased more than 2 percent, you are making financial progress. In fact, this may be worthy of a simple chart you could make on your computer or by hand. As long as the line is going up, you're making progress. When gross income falls but does not quickly recover, you need to pay particular attention. This means you may be heading for a personal recession.

Cash flow

Your cash flow is your gross income for a set period of time—say for a month or the year—minus your total outgo for that same period. You can see that your gross income could increase while your cash flow sinks if your spending is increasing at a faster rate than your income. Locking eyeballs with the reality of your cash flow can be shocking and quite possibly just the jolt you need to rein in your spending.

Now that you know how to create a monthly spending plan you're on your way to having all you need to create a really great Cash Flow Statement. This is a report that shows all the income for the year and all the outgo. What came in and what happened to it?

Businesses rely heavily on cash-flow statements in projecting growth and boosting profits. You are no less important than a business, so an annual cash-flow statement will become a valuable tool as you better manage your money.

Using the information from your twelve monthly records, fill in the cash-flow form, which is divided into three categories: Income, Fixed Expenses, and Variable Expenses.

Ideally, your exact income should equal your exact outgo which means you've been able to account for every dollar that passed through your hands for that period of time. Don't panic if you can't be that exact. The fact that you've come this far is remarkable. Besides, I don't know anyone who could be precise to the penny over an entire year. It's a fine goal, so keep reaching for it.

Net worth

Simply put, your net worth is the amount of money you would have left if you sold everything you own and used that money to pay off everything that you owe. Creating your first Statement of Net Worth will take some time and effort. I want to encourage you to do this because it will give you amazing insight into many things, such as the way some things lose value quickly. A case in point might be a new vehicle you purchased two years ago

Cash-Flow Statement

As of _____

INCOME

Gross Salaries		*$
Dividend Income		
Interest Income		
Savings		
Other		
Total Income		*$

OUTGO

Savings		
Giving		
Investments		
Taxes		
Mortgage Payments		
Debt Payments		
Insurance Premiums		
Food		
Transportation		
Clothing/Personal Care		
Entertainment/Vacations		
Medical/Dental		
Utilities/Household Expenses		
Miscellaneous		
Total Outgo		*$

*These two amounts should be the same.

that today is worth less as an asset than the amount you owe on it, which is a liability.

Your first statement of net worth will be your benchmark, a reference point. Next year you will be able to compare your financial picture with this year's statement to see the changes. Kind of like a baseline mammogram.

There are only two ways you can improve your net worth: increase assets and decrease liabilities.

If you are married, your net worth statement should be the financial condition of you as a couple in one joint statement.

The information you will need to gather is the current market value of all of your assets and the exact figure of your liabilities. Assets are anything you own of value, including cash or cash equivalents, investments, and use-assets such as your home, cars, and personal possessions of value. You'll probably have to take an inventory to gather the information you'll need for preparation of your financial statement. Don't get too detailed, however.

Cash and cash equivalents are cash in your possession right now and money in checking accounts, savings and money market accounts that you could make liquid (turn into cash) in about three weeks. Investments would be stocks, bonds, mutual funds, savings bonds, and so on, which would take longer to make liquid.

When assessing your personal property, arrive at a dollar figure for which you can reasonably sell everything you own in the next ninety days. If you have a substantial amount of jewelry, collections, or art (say a market value of over ten thousand dollars) those should be listed separately. Otherwise, come up with one figure for personal property.

Next list all your debts. Be honest and exact. If you don't know for sure, call the lender and ask. Come up with a total number for unsecured debt (credit cards, installment loans, personal loans, student loans), and another for any automobiles and your real estate mortgages.

Your net worth statement is an important tool because it helps:

- Check and measure your financial progress in relation to your financial goals. Think of it as a financial "growth chart."

- Make decisions about acquiring assets and taking on liabilities in the future.

- Estimate how well-off your family would be if you were suddenly taken from them.

- Determine your need for life and property insurance and adjustments you need to make in your coverage.

- Give an estimate of what your income will be during your retirement.

A net worth statement does not care about income. In fact there is not even a place to record your annual salary. A net worth statement doesn't care how much you spend on food, clothes or education. What your statement reveals is how much of your hard-earned income you keep. It confirms our belief that it doesn't really matter how much money you make. You are worth what you saved, not the money you made. What matters is what you do with your money.

There are two major categories on a net worth statement: Assets and Liabilities—what you own and what you owe. When you deduct what you owe from what you own, the result will be your Net Worth.

Assets

Your assets are your material possessions—everything from cash to investments, clothes to cars. Even those things you are in the process of paying off and do not yet own outright are considered assets.

Assets are divided into two categories: Appreciating assets and depreciating assets.

Appreciating assets are things you own that become more

valuable over time. Everything else is losing value and therefore depreciating.

Investments such as retirement accounts and stock market holdings are appreciating assets because they have the likelihood of gaining in value over time. Savings and cash come under the heading of appreciating assets, so does real estate. Certain collectibles appreciate, but be careful here. You want "market confirmation" of the values you set for your appreciating assets. You may believe your Beanie Baby® collection is worth a lot more than what you could realistically sell it for next weekend.

Depreciating assets lose or decrease in value over time. Clothes, furniture, cars, boats, and electronics would fall into this category of depreciating assets.

On your net worth statement list each of your Appreciating Assets with a corresponding value for each. Example: If your home would sell for $200,000 on today's market and you have a $100,000 mortgage, list it as $200,000 under your Appreciating Assets.

This is where you will include the current value of your retirement accounts, today's market value of certificates, stocks, bonds and mutual fund shares. Use actual cash figures for cash on hand and in checking and savings accounts.

Example: If your savings account shows $1,273 today, enter that amount exactly. If you have $500 in your savings, enter it separately.

Include money owed to you as an asset, but only if you are certain of repayment. Example: If you lent $1,000 to a friend at 8 percent interest and he has already repaid $300, enter this as $700 under Appreciating Assets. Do not value potential interest you will earn.

To find the current value of your investments look for market quotes in a current newspaper or by going to a website like *Yahoo.com* and checking the day's financial markets. You can get the current day's value for each of the stocks and mutual funds you own by simply typing in the ticker symbol which you can also look up at the site.

Other possessions, such as your cars, big screen TV, boat, clothes, jewelry and household goods, are depreciating assets because while they have value they are becoming less valuable with time. Unless your car is a rare collector's item (in which case it would be an appreciating asset), it is worth less today than it was yesterday. In fact if you bought it new, it was worth 20 percent less the day after you bought it due to depreciation.

It is customary to group assets into categories like "Real Estate," or "Personal Property" which would include your clothes and household goods. Some experts suggest an estimate of $10,000 current market value for personal property including furniture, clothes, tools and all other household items of a typical two-adult household. You may wish to use that figure or determine your own. If you have a lot of valuable furniture or many collectibles you can list them separately.

Liabilities

When it comes to a net worth statement, debt is debt. We make no differentiation between secured and unsecured debt. Any amount you owe another person or entity should be accounted for under "liabilities."

Using the illustration on page 170 as your example, list your liabilities. These are obligations like mortgages, home equity loans, car loans, automobile leases, student loans, personal loans, court-mandated child support (up to one year's worth), leases, contracts for things like wireless devices, gym membership contracts—anything for which you have an obligation to pay.

Subtract your Total Liabilities from Total Assets. The result is your current Net Worth.

Your Net Worth tells a story. It doesn't lie, it doesn't deceive. The last number—the bottom line—reveals how much of your income you've managed to keep. If that is a negative number, you've managed to spend more than you've earned, relying on credit to fill in that gap. Or you can think of it this way: You've been spending all you earned, plus a lot you haven't even earned yet.

What you see on your net worth statement is your financial condition as of today. If you are discouraged by what you see let me encourage you: You have control over this situation. As helpless or hopeless as you may feel right now, the truth is: It's up to you. This is a picture you can change beginning now.

Take another look at your net worth statement. Focus on one of your debts, like a credit-card debt. Imagine that you will reduce that balance by $5 when you send your payment tomorrow. That will immediately increase your Net Worth by $5. Five dollars here, ten dollars there is the way to get on board with changing your financial picture.

Perhaps the most important thing you can learn from this chapter: Reducing debt increases Net Worth dollar for dollar, in the same way it increases as you increase your assets. A repaid debt is a good investment.

Your assignment

Just as soon as practical, prepare your net worth statement. Make a form like the one that follows. Do this work as accurately as possible. To inflate figures or cheat by excluding liabilities only hurts you. You need to know where you are so that you will be able to measure how you are doing as you begin to debt-proof your life.

You will be creating a benchmark against which to measure your future progress. That is going to have a positive effect on your determination to become a better caretaker of your money. (The example compares two non-consecutive years for illustration only.) This should be at least an annual effort.

It is going to be exciting to plot your financial growth. Even your smallest efforts to repay debt and save money are going to count when they will show up in black and white.

Net Worth Statement –2-Year Comparison				
	As of Aug. 1, 2006		As of Aug. 1, 2007	
Assets - Appreciating				
Cash in Checking	12		1,808	
Savings Accounts	0		10,000	
Retirement 401k and IRAs	804		2,765	
House	132,000		175,000	
Stocks, bonds, funds	0		575	
Other	12,000		15,000	
Total Appreciating Assets		$ 144,816		$ 205,148
Assets - Depreciating				
Personal Property	10,000		10,000	
Auto - 2004 Chevy Truck	24,000		16,000	
Auto - 2000 Acura	4,000		1,000	
Jet Ski	2,300		750	
Total Depreciating Assets		40,300		27,750
TOTAL ASSETS		$ 185,116		$ 232,898
Liabilities				
Home mortgage	122,000		112,000	
HEL (home equity loan)	0		5,000	
Student loans	32,000		30,000	
Credit-card debt	18,900		2,000	
Loan from 401k	0		0	
Loan from parents	4,000		0	
Past due utility bills	223		0	
Jet Ski	745		0	
Doctors	1,900		0	
Hospitals	545		0	
Truck loan	23,000		17,000	
TOTAL LIABILITIES		- $ 203,313		- $ 166,000
NET WORTH		<$ 18,197>		$ 66,898

Chapter 14

The Least You Need to Know About Getting What You Pay For

> *"Your objective is to reeducate sellers, teach them that
> your money isn't theirs without your consent. If they've cheated
> to get your money, don't let them keep it."*
> *– Donna McCrohan, author, "Get What You Pay for or Don't Pay at All"*

I t was brilliant. There's no other way to describe the way syndicated talk-show radio host Rich Buhler ended a particularly difficult call, "Just remember this: Always remain a fragrance, never become an odor." Over the years, that little piece of advice has stuck with me like static cling.

When I was growing up I didn't fully understand the concept although I was rebuked again and again for "your attitude," "that tone of voice!" and "it's not what you say, but the way you say it." As motherhood was thrust upon me—you know, that time in life when you start saying the things your parents said— I came into full awareness of this concept.

It's not necessarily what we say, but the way we say it. One version leaves a fragrance, the other projects an odor. Fragrance leave us yearning for more while odors send us running for cover. Time and again since first considering this fragrance/odor thing, I've been able to look back and determine what went wrong—where the negotiations broke down. It wasn't what I said to my parents that was particularly offensive but the way I said it.

Personality traits that I label as enthusiasm and zeal can easily be misconstrued as criticism and control. What I say can be taken in the wrong way. When that happens I'm afraid I give off an "odor" that does absolutely nothing to endear me to the person with whom I'm dealing. But somehow, this idea that I might be spewing forth an offending "odor" has a way of engaging my pause button, which gives me a moment to catch my breath so I can quickly reevaluate and hopefully soften up a little bit. And so it is with this whole subject of getting what you pay for. If you know how to behave with fragrance, charm, and dignity, you'll get the results you deserve every time.

Your Reasonable Expectations

Contrary to what the old rock and roll song stated about getting satisfaction, I believe that with the right attitude, the correct information, and reliable resources, it is possible to be satisfied with your purchase of goods and services. It's all a matter of knowing what to say and how to say it.

As consumers in this great country, we have the right to expect quality products and services at fair prices. We have the right to receive what we pay for and for sellers to stand behind their products if a problem develops.

When you think about it, it's not exactly unreasonable to expect to get what you pay for. We the faithful consumers are a necessary part of this country's economy. And as responsible stewards of the many resources entrusted to us by God, I believe we have an obligation to make sure we get what we pay for.

Confrontation has never been high on my list of things I love to do. There was a time in my life that even when I purchased something that turned out to be clearly defective I would worry that the store owner wouldn't agree with me or wouldn't believe me, insisting that the product was fine when it left the store, so I must have caused the damage. And the idea of returning an item simply because the color turned out to be wrong or I just changed my mind intimidated me beyond belief. Somewhere deep down inside of me I just didn't want to give the sales clerk an opportunity to yell at me or announce over the loud speaker to the entire community that some woman up here has the un-mitigated gall to change her mind.

This particular aversion cost me a lot of money over the years. My compulsive nature and propensity to buy everything in sight, particularly if it was on sale (which for a shopaholic always con-firms God's blessing on the purchase and His providential sup-plying of need), coupled with my fear of returning were a deadly combination of behaviors. At this point in my life I'd just as soon not know how many brand-new items—some defective, some not—I've given away or thrown out simply because I was too em-barrassed, too lazy, or just couldn't be bothered to take them back.

The good news is that most sellers make a concerted effort to settle customer complaints in a satisfactory manner. Many even go beyond the minimum required by federal consumer-protec-tion laws, not only because it's the right thing to do, but be-cause it's a great way to keep us as loyal, returning customers.

And guess what? I observed the way financially responsible women live; and through mimicking their behaviors in this area of making sure I always get what I pay for, I've changed. I've learned how to practice this habit of reasonable expectation—not with a demanding demeanor or threatening attitude, but just a gentle expectation that sellers are not entitled to my money without my full consent.

The more I exercise this new behavior, the more cautious I become at the point of purchase. I make selections more care-fully, think things through, and actually take time to make de-cisions. Because I know the consequences of an inappropriate purchase may include the dreaded return to the store for a re-fund or acceptable adjustment, making the best decision the first time around has become much more important than it used to be.

A Short History of Consumer Protection

In the late 1800s, increased industrialization in this country provided the opportunity for many new kinds of businesses to advertise and sell their products nationwide. As you can well imagine, along with this unprecedented growth of business came the issue of consumer problems.

In 1938 when over one hundred people died after using a new liquid sulfa drug, a law was enacted requiring manufacturers to prove the safety of new drugs to the Federal Drug Administration before putting them on the market.

World War II diverted attention from the growing lack of consumer protection. The issue didn't attract interest again until the 1960s. During that decade new programs to protect the public were put into action and existing programs were improved. In 1967 the Consumer Federation of America was formed to serve as an umbrella organization of consumer, cooperative, and labor groups.

About this time Ralph Nader's book, *Unsafe at Any Speed*, was published, and he quickly emerged as the leader of a wide range of reform efforts. Many young people volunteered to work in his organization, and under his leadership they participated in research, writing, and lobbying to improve consumer protection.

During the 1960s and 1970s many new laws were enacted to protect consumers. Among them were the Motor Vehicle Safety Act (1966), the Truth in Lending Act (1969), the Consumer Product Safety Act (1972), the Toy Safety Act (1969), and legislation to strengthen the Federal Trade Commission.

Even with the rise in consumer protectionism and awareness, too many of us seem to accept that time is more important than money—that it's better to be cheated out of a few bucks or more than to waste time going after it. Most of us, if we complain at all, do so to friends and neighbors but usually let the guilty company off the hook because it's simply not worth the bother.

According to Technical Assistance Research Programs only 4 percent of us let a business know when we're dissatisfied with its product or service.

A new awareness in consumer rights has emerged in the past few years. Consumers have been hit broadside by a rough economy and new trends toward frugality, and are much more anxious to exercise their rights to fairness.

Complaining with Fragrance

Probably the most important part of getting what you pay for is to keep your receipts in some kind of an organized fashion. It's not as difficult as you might imagine. Any method will do, provided you can easily put your hands on the receipt you need. If something you purchased came with an owner's manual or paperwork, staple the receipt to the front. Always take a moment to write on the receipt a brief description of the item since many receipts carry only a stock number or abbreviation that may be completely indecipherable six months from now. Receipts should be kept for at least a year, and longer for goods or services that have a reasonable life expectancy of a longer period of time.

Think of the problem-resolution process as a pyramid with a set of ascending stairs. Most problems are readily resolved at ground level where the pyramid is the largest. Some situations may require you to climb up a step or two, while more difficult situations may require going much closer to the top. However, the times you will have to climb even close to the top of the pyramid will likely be few.

When dealing with a salesperson or representative, always bear in mind that person deserves your highest respect. He or she has the right to be treated as a person with intelligence and feelings, as a person who may very well be working under difficult conditions with an unreasonable supervisor, or as a person who occasionally has a bad day just as you do.

Next, always deal reasonably and don't be rude. Consider that this stranger with whom you are dealing may very well be the visitor sitting beside you in church next Sunday!

Before beginning the complaint-resolution process, have the following things clear in your mind.

❖ The exact nature of the problem.

❖ Specifically how you wish it to be remedied.

❖ A specific time frame in which you expect the problem will be completely solved.

❖ Your next step if you are unable to find resolution at this level.

Principle: Take care of problems before leaving the store or while the service person or contractor is still on the job. Perhaps you discover before leaving the restaurant that the waitress has made a mathematical error in your bill, or the painter missed a section of baseboard in the hall bathroom. Whatever the problem, gently take care of it prior to making full payment. Remember you have a right to only pay for what you get.

Principle: Approach the highest-ranking employee with your problem, and with great dignity and grace seek satisfactory resolution. If this doesn't work, ask for the name and location of the regional manager or a phone number for customer service. Record the name and title of the person with whom you've been dealing along with the date of this confrontation. Hint: When approaching in person, be careful of how you're dressed. As unfair as it might be, people do make snap judgments based on appearance. This alone might influence what they believe to be the value in keeping you as a customer, to say nothing of the legitimacy of your problem. This is not the time to look like a mess.

Principle: The next level is the telephone call. Before you make the call, rehearse the facts of your situation. Don't dump on the receptionist. Try to speak with the highest-ranking person at this location. If you are not successful at this level, take the name and title of the person(s) with whom you spoke and record them along with the date. If you're successful in having your complaint resolved, ask that the resolution be put in writing and mailed to you. If this is not forthcoming, follow up with your own letter outlining your understanding of the terms of the agreement and a summary of the conversation.

Principle: If your complaint has not been resolved by now, a letter is your next course of action. Letters are great because you get an opportunity to collect your thoughts and arrange them orderly and logically. You have a record of what you've "said" and no one can interrupt. Be sure to include a clear and simple statement of the problem, how you've attempted resolution to date, the resolution you expect, and the date by which you expect it to be accomplished. A typed or computer-printed letter is preferable; however, a neatly handwritten letter can be just as effective.

In the letter include your name, address, and daytime phone number. Make your letter brief and to the point. Include all important facts about your purchase including the date and place where you made the purchase and any information you can give about the product or service, such as serial or model numbers or specific type of service. State exactly what you want done about the problem and how long you are willing to wait to get it resolved. Be reasonable. Include photocopies of all documents regarding your problem. Avoid writing an angry, sarcastic, or threatening letter. The person reading your letter probably was not responsible for your problem but may be very helpful in resolving it. Keep a copy of your letter.

About a year ago I purchased a round-trip airplane ticket. When it arrived in the mail, the envelope contained two identical tickets with identical seat assignments and identical numbering. I immediately called to point out the error only to be informed that I'd been charged for both tickets and neither was refundable. Can you believe that? A computer glitch that was not my fault should be charged to my account?

The airline was completely unreasonable. I have fragrantly fought this now for about six months. Finally, they agreed this was their error and promised they would refund the price of the duplicate ticket. Oh, I received a refund all right, but it was for only one-half the full amount. Obviously the concept of round-trip eludes this particular company. Eventually I did receive a full refund.

Whenever it's important to prove that you sent something or sent it by a certain date, invest a few extra dollars in mailing it certified or registered, return receipt requested.

Keep a good paper trail from the beginning. This means copies of everything including receipts, your letters, letters you've received, canceled checks, and so on. Copies of contemporaneous notes will be valuable as well.

If you do not receive full satisfaction, you need to seek third-party assistance. I suggest you contact your state's Consumer Protection office, which you can easily find on the Internet by searching "Consumer Protection Office" plus your state.

You as a consumer are well protected by laws that are meant to prevent fraud and provide consumers with an advocate.

The issue of consumer complaints and satisfaction, like anything, can be taken to an inappropriate extreme.

I first learned of one particular woman on television and have since followed her through a newsletter she publishes. While her basic philosophy is exemplary (spend less, invest more), I believe she's taken this particular subject of consumer satisfaction way too far. Her diligence with money borders on obsession, to the point that she plans on at least three thousand dollars additional income per year to be derived from her complaint proceeds. She purposely purchases with complaints and refunds in mind. Her contention is that full satisfaction is impossible to achieve because she can always find something about which to complain.

The secret of her "success," she proudly beams, is in making her complaint after the item has been consumed. I don't call that success. I call that dishonest manipulation. In a way she might as well be shoplifting because in her exuberance to get a fair deal, she's crossed the line into thievery.

The key here is to stay true—to not complain when there is no problem, but to be courageous when there is. Personally I can't think of a better way to become good stewards of the resources we have than making sure each dollar spent is spent well. By eliminating purchasing mistakes and following up when we are truly not satisfied, we will dramatically affect the bottom line of our financial statements. So be brave, become a documentation fiend, and always deal fragrantly.

Sample Letter

Your Address
Your City, State, Zip Code
Date

Appropriate Person
Company Name
Street Address
City, State, Zip Code.

Dear Sirs (or name):

Last week I purchased a [name of product including serial and model number]. I made this purchase at [location, date, and other pertinent information].

Unfortunately your product [or service] has not performed satisfactorily because [describe problem with product or service]. I would appreciate your [state specific action you desire].

Enclosed are copies of my records [receipts, guarantees, warranties, canceled checks, contracts, and any other necessary documentation].

I am looking forward to your reply and resolution of my problem and will wait three weeks before seeking third-party assistance. Contact me at the above address or by phone at (home or office numbers).

Sincerely,

Your name and signature

Chapter 15

The Least You Need to Know About Preparing for the Future

" ...Give me neither poverty nor riches! Give me just enough to satisfy my needs. For if I grow rich, I may deny you and say, 'Who is the LORD?' And if I am too poor, I may steal and thus insult God's holy name."
– Proverbs 30:8-9

My heart was broken when I finished reading a letter from Betty. She related how she and her husband, both octogenarians, struggle from one day to the next—not because of physical limitations, but because of their financial disabilities. They led a very affluent lifestyle during their younger years and just assumed, along with millions of their peers, that everything would work out once they retired. Now that they are trying to exist on their social security benefits, they've had a rude awakening.

Not only must they continue making payments on their home

because they failed to pay off their mortgage during their years of employment, they are carrying tremendous credit card debt as a result of trying to survive day by day. Their dream was that when they retired they'd travel. They would pursue hobbies and do all the things they'd put off during the years they were raising a family and building careers.

Because Betty and her husband are too old to be employed, too unemployed to qualify for more credit, too "well off" to receive public assistance, and too proud to turn to their children for help—they really have no options. I could feel the tears between the lines as she begged me to warn others of the need to prepare well for retirement. "At the time of life when we should be enjoying ourselves the most, we're sitting at a dead-end waiting to die."

Betty's letter became a personal wake-up call for Harold and me. I'll admit it: Retirement was not something on which I chose to dwell. It sounds so old! Why should we worry about it now? There will be plenty of time to prepare later, I argued. And then I was hit by this truth: The winter season of my life will arrive on time, whether I'm prepared or not. Clearly, being prepared beats the alternative.

Planning for the future has filled me with excitement and wonder. Excitement because of all the technology and medical resources available, and wonder for why I didn't start sooner.

The bad news is that increasing life expectancies mean most people will outlive their retirement dollars. The good news is that running out of money is rarely a problem for the wise steward who plans ahead and anticipates retirement.

A Second Lifetime to Enjoy

We are certainly among the most fortunate in the history of the world. As American women, we can expect to live nearly one-third more years in retirement than men of the same age. And we have the knowledge and resources available to make sure we are in the best of health in order to enjoy those extra years.

If you compare yourself to your great-grandmother, you can

plan to enjoy an extended life because a woman's life expectancy has nearly doubled over the last century. What an exciting prospect. It's like getting the gift of a second lifetime. But don't underestimate the fact that making your second lifetime live up to your dreams is going to take a good deal of planning, and the sooner the better.

Your probable life span

Of course none of us can know how long we will live, but we can make some educated predictions based on statistics and probabilities. Your insurance agent or a simple google search will help you locate a current ordinary mortality table. Using your present age, health, and physical condition, predict how many years you will live. If you have a strong constitution the semi-weird website *DeathClock.com* will make a specific prediction based on only a couple of pieces of information.

Of course our days are numbered—no one but God knows how long we have to live—and statistics can help us know how to plan. Here's the bottom line: You do not want to outlive your money.

Your projected retirement income

The first place to start in projecting your retirement income is the Social Security Administration. Go to *SSA.gov* or call 800-772-1213 to request your Social Security Statement—a concise, easy-to-read personal record of the earnings on which you have paid Social Security taxes during your working years and a summary of the estimated benefits you and your family may receive as a result of those earnings. This is important for several reasons:

• You'll be able to see if all your employment has been included in your SSI account.

• You'll have an opportunity to correct any errors (the agency seems to have a very high goof rate).

• You will be able to project your Social Security benefits in retirement if you continue contributing at your present rate.

The Secret is Balance

In Jesus' Sermon on the Mount recorded in Matthew 6, we are told to stop worrying about the future. In fact, he gives us an example in flowers—lilies to be exact—to illustrate how God wonderfully cares and provides for our needs. Like the lilies of the field, we are to be beautiful, not toiling and fretting about how we will be cared for.

Now pop on over to Proverbs 6 and we're admonished to not be lazy but to take our cues from the lowly ant who works hard all summer to gather food for the winter to come.

While you might at first see these two passages of Scripture to be contradictory, they aren't at all! There is no doubt that God keeps his promises to provide for our needs, both for today and for the years to come. I'm certain that if I could open the floor to discussion, we'd be here for months or even years listening to all the personal testimonies and moving stories of how God has provided for us in small and even miraculous ways.

So do we show a lack of faith if we concern ourselves with preparations for our financial future? Not at all. In fact, it delights God when we are good stewards with what he gives us to manage. And the more he can trust us, the more he will trust us to care for even more.

Look, God knows how many days and years are ahead for each one of us. He's not limited by some kind of calendar that is divided up into equal pay periods. I do not believe God is providing for you right now just the amount of money that you need only to get through next Friday. He sees the future, he knows what's ahead and he's entrusting you now with the money you're going to need then. He's already providing for the needs you will have that you don't even know about. The way not to worry about your future is to be wise, by acknowledging the need to put aside some part of everything you receive so you'll be ready for winter.

By being responsible now during the summer of your life you will be prepared when winter comes. Only a foolish person would consciously spend all she has now and then head into that season of her life with no financial provisions.

We will outlive the men

Statistically speaking, if you have a man in your life, you are going to outlive him. And if you don't, well that makes things even more certain that at some time in your life as a woman you will be solely responsible for your support, your finances and your care. Get used to the idea. Women outlive men.

Now that we have that straight, let's boil your needs down to just two categories: Money and documents. You need both.

The Documents You Need

A will

While you absolutely need a will, in the big picture having a will is only slightly better than having nothing when it comes to preparing for your future. But you must start here. The purpose of a will is to tell your heirs and the government how you want your estate (the sum total of what you leave on earth) distributed to your loved ones after your death. Your will also says who you want to become the legal guardian of your minor children.

If you die without a will, the laws of the state will decide all of the above for you—including who will care for your minor children.

A revocable living trust

A will and a trust go hand in hand—you need both. The purpose of a living trust is to allow your assets to be passed to your heirs without going through the often expensive, confusing and long process of probate where the state settles your affairs and distributes your assets. That it is revocable means you can change it any time you want. It's not in stone, but it is in effect.

Your revocable living trust (*revocable* means that you can change it at anytime in the future, as opposed to an *irrevocable* trust that is set in stone) needs also to contain an incapacity clause, which allows the trustee you select to make your financial decisions if you do not die but for some reason become incapacitated.

Durable power of attorney for health care

This is a document in which you name a person you wish to make your healthcare and medical decisions if you become unable to do this for yourself. We are not talking just old age here. You could be hit by a bus this afternoon, rendering you incapable for a period of time or for much longer. Who do you want making your medical decisions? That's what a durable attorney for health care does—it names that person and gives that person your permission to act on your behalf.

How to Get These Documents

The quickest way to get all three documents (or if you have some of them already, to get them reviewed) is to make an appointment with an attorney. Ask friends or relatives for a recommendation.

There are also do-it-yourself options. I highly recommend Nolo Press (*Nolo.com*), a terrific resource that produces do-it-yourself legal books and software that reduce the need for people to hire lawyers for simple legal matters such as making wills or writing business partnership contracts.

The Money You Will Need in Retirement

For most women retirement holds a great deal of mystery. And for those who do not work outside the home, it can be worse than that.

Where will you get your income if your spouse stops working for any number of reasons?

If you have worked all your life, are you guaranteed a retirement income? Will Social Security provide the income you need?

Uncertainty about the future is common among women, but that does not have to be the case for you. You can become certain and financially confident about the years that lay ahead. This requires two things: Knowledge and action.

Here is the underlying principle. The longer you have to save, the less money you will need to contribute. Refer back to compounding interest in chapter 7. If you start saving for retirement early, it's a lot cheaper because of interest and compounding growth. Another way to put it: Save early, save often and save consistently.

The pretax advantage

Whether you know it as gross versus net, or pretax versus after-tax, you know that when you get a paycheck what you see in your hand is not the same amount of money you earned. What you earned is the gross amount, what you get is known as net or your after-tax dollars. The difference? Taxes and all the withholding required by the federal and state government.

One of the best gifts you will ever get from the government is the provision that allows you to save and invest for retirement using your pretax dollars.

Just for illustration purposes, let's say your paycheck is $1,000 gross per week. Of course you don't get all of that, but something closer to about $750 or about 75 cents after tax for each dollar earned.

However, if you are willing to save your money into a qualified savings plan, the government allows you to save pretax dollars. They say something like, "If you will put that $1 into a qualified retirement account, we'll let you invest and benefit from the 25 cents that belongs to us and when you do retire, we'll take those 25 cents then." Well, that's the simplified version, but it gives you a good idea of how a retirement savings plan works.

Your ability to invest your dollars before taxes are withheld is huge. This is your ace in the hole, the secret for how you will be able to build a retirement nest egg—provided you will just keep your hands off the money as it grows. But you need to know where to find these qualified accounts and how to set up your retirement savings.

Retirement plan at work

If you are employed, chances are good that your employer offers a retirement plan. Corporations offer 401(k) plans; nonprofits like schools, hospitals and churches can offer 403(b) plans. There are others as well that go by the acronyms TSA and TSP (for tax-sheltered annuity and thrift savings plan, respectively). Which type of retirement plan your employer offers is not important right now. That you are signed up is what matters. You do that immediately if you have not already. For now, I will just refer to all pretax retirement plans as "401(k)s".

As of this writing, the most you can invest in your 401(k) is $15,500 per year unless you are over fifty years old, in which case you can save an additional "catch-up" amount of $5,000 for a total of $20,500. If you are married, both you and your spouse may each be able to put $15,500 in pretax dollars into your respective employer's 401(k) plans.

Employer match

Here's another reason you need to sign up now for your employer's retirement plan: company match. Many companies will contribute some of their money to your account either as a flat out gift, or a matching gift. This does not count toward the limitation above for how much you can contribute. And you do not pay taxes on this money until you retire and or you take that money out of your account.

Employers are not required to offer a matching or other contribution, so find out the terms of your company's plan. If your employer does offer to match a portion of your contribution and you are not accepting it, you are walking away from free money. This is just one more reason to find out as soon as possible which retirement plans are available to you.

Retirement saving on your own

There are ways that you can get in on the pretax savings benefit if you are not employed or simply do not want to put all of your eggs into your company's retirement plan. If the latter, I strongly suggest that you participate at least to the matching point so that you do not leave money on the table.

If you are a non-working spouse or a stay-at-home mom or do not work outside your home, you can and you should still be contributing to a retirement account.

Traditional IRA

There are several types of qualified individual retirement accounts (IRAs) that you can set up, invest in and manage on your own. The number of pretax dollars you can contribute each year depends on whether your employer offers a plan at work and how much money you earn each year. But don't worry about that right yet. Let's get the big picture clear first, and then we'll deal with those details.

A traditional IRA is similar to a 401(k) in that you invest pretax dollars. When it's time to withdraw money in retirement you must pay taxes on the money which was not previously taxed, as well as taxes on the gain. The thought here is that you will likely be in a lower tax bracket at that time than the one you are in now during your earning years, so you will come out ahead.

Roth IRA

This is a fairly new type of IRA retirement account that works differently, but in a very beneficial way. In a Roth IRA, you contribute your after-tax dollars. No break there. But here's where it gets very beneficial. When you withdraw the money later, you will not have to pay taxes on any of it. None. Nada. This is huge, especially for those of you who will be starting early, contributing regularly and allowing the miracle of compounding interest to kick in.

Where to get started

Go online or call a reputable brokerage company that offers retirement accounts and ask to speak with an customer service rep. Here are two companies for your consideration: T. Rowe Price (*TRowePrice.com*; 800-541-6066) or Vanguard (*Vanguard. com*; 800-523-1036). Tell the rep you are interested in opening an individual retirement account and you need to know the limitations and qualifiers to do so.

At this time, Vanguard requires $3,000 minimum to open an account, while T. Rowe Price will open an account for you provided you agree to $50 automatic deposits each month.

Get your list of questions together, then just pick up the phone. Your confidence will soar with each new thing you learn about investing money now for your retirement later.

Non-Qualified Investments

When we speak of a "qualified" investment this refers to a plan or program approved by the IRS that allows you to invest pretax dollars or has some other approved benefit like that of a Roth IRA. But you are not limited to only qualified investments. You can and probably will invest in many other ways once you have maxed out your qualified investment options.

Chapter 16

Six-Week Plan of Action

"Little drops of water wear down big stones."
– Russian Proverb

O nce you can do something for twenty-one consecutive repetitions, whether it's exercising, learning an instrument, or practicing new behaviors with money, you will be well on your way to establishing a new habit. Another cycle of twenty-one repetitions, or six weeks if repeated on a daily basis, will establish the new behavior as a lifelong behavior.

You will be able to take the following guidelines and apply them to your particular set of circumstances. During this six-week period you should have the opportunity to balance your checkbook twice—which will be a good start, but hardly sufficient repetition to establish that particular activity as a habit. There are many things that are not done on a daily basis but that you will want to include in your list of new habits to learn.

I am a believer in the value of journaling. I recommend the next six weeks include intensive writing on your part. Find a notebook or journal that you can keep in a private and secure place. A three-ring binder works well and will accommodate your journaling, spending records, and spending plans.

Spending Records

It's time to start keeping a daily spending record. Think of this as counting—counting what comes in and what goes out. The journey to financial clarity begins by simply counting. Start right away regardless of where you are in the calendar month and continue every day for the next six weeks (at the very least). Follow the instructions in chapter 13 for keeping a Daily Spending Record, Weekly Spending Reports, and the Monthly Spending Record. You will have an opportunity at some point during this time to prepare your first Monthly Spending Plan.

Week One:
Choose Abstinence and Commitment

Abstinence. No, you haven't stumbled into a twelve-step recovery program. Not that I have anything against the twelve-step programs. In fact for those who have severe spending problems, Debtor's Anonymous is highly recommended.

Abstinence simply means to keep oneself back, to refrain voluntarily. Abstinence is the primary tool for getting out of debt. So for those who have unsecured debt, voluntarily abstaining from incurring any new debt for the next six weeks will be a challenge indeed. First, separate yourself from the credit cards. At the very least, move them from your wallet or purse to a place in your home where they will be secure.

While it is not advisable for you to cancel credit-card accounts on which you carry a balance (the bank would likely raise your interest rate to the max if you were to do that), you can "close" these accounts to yourself. Put that one all-purpose credit card that you've had the longest into a safe place. Now cut up all the others. It's not going to be easy, but you need to do that if for no other reason than to affirm your commitment to get out of debt.

Tip: Freeze the one you choose to keep in a container of water. Keep this credit card "safe" in your freezer. You'll know where the card is, and you'll also feel pretty silly standing there at the sink waiting for it to thaw so you can make a compulsive purchase.

Abstinence is a simple tool, but do not underestimate it. This week's focus is on not incurring debt, don't beat yourself up right now about repayment.

You may even want to devote a section of your journal to abstinence and start listing and writing about other things you will refrain from doing. Ask God to bring to your mind those habits that are hindering your walk of faith and journey to financial freedom.

Commitment. In your journal, make a written commitment to the amount of money you will begin giving and the amount you will pay to yourself. Select a savings vehicle (savings account, sugar bowl, mutual fund) into which you will deposit your savings.

Week Two:
Explore Your Belief System

In your journal, write down your fundamental beliefs about money. Refer to chapter 4 to see if any of the beliefs described there strike a chord.

Make a heading, "My Money Training." Write your memories of situations involving the way money was dealt with in your family.

Follow this with "My adult money beliefs." How did those events from your childhood shape what you think about money today? What did each event teach you about the way you should or shouldn't think about money? You should be able to come up with three or four of these applicable memories. The more you write the sooner you'll see a connection between what you learned about money and how you behave with it today.

Answer the following questions as a way of getting in touch with your money beliefs:

How much money did your family have?

Were you poor? Rich?

Have you since discovered that your family was richer (or poorer) than you thought when you were a child?

When you really wanted something as a child, who did you ask? Why?

Did you have about the same, more, or less money than your childhood friends?

Whose job was it to earn the money for your family?

Whose job was it to spend the money?

Who made the financial decisions?

What false beliefs, if any, did you find in your personal search? Write about the correct and healthy beliefs you have.

These questions are meant to jump-start your memory and help you sift through all the money training you've had from your earliest recollection.

Identify your false money beliefs. Write them down and commit to removing them from your life by replacing them with solid values.

Finish the week by making a fresh new list of your personal money beliefs.

Week Three:
Take Stock

Values. Using the work you did last week in determining your money beliefs, what values will become your life guide for handling money?

What new money attitudes will become an outward manifestation of these values?

Inventory. This week prepare a written inventory of your financial matters. Here is a list of the information you need:

Your debts. For each non-mortgage debt you have, write down the following three things about that debt:

What is the current total outstanding balance?

What is the interest rate?

What is the current minimum monthly payment?

If you continue making only the minimum payment each month and incur no new debt, how many monthly payments will you have to make until the debt is completely paid?

Do some real soul searching in this exercise. Think back to debts you might have but that you've tried to forget, like that thousand bucks you borrowed from your sister five years ago. You need to pay it back. Write it down.

Your assets. Make a list of the things you own that have a market value. Be as detailed as you want.

Week Four:
Find Your Balance

By now you should have received a bank statement for your checking account. Refer to chapter 13 and balance it following the instructions. If it takes all week, so what? Cut yourself a little slack and stick with it. It will balance.

Prepare your Cash Flow Statement. If you do not have information for the past year (I would be very surprised if you do to be quite frank), prepare this statement for the current period, even if it is only the past week or two.

Prepare your Net Worth Statement to determine your current net worth. In the event you have a negative net worth, meaning you owe more than you own, don't do anything rash. Just face the truth and commit to getting that situation reversed as soon as possible.

Week Five:
Formulate a Get-Out-of-Debt Plan

Using the information from last week, make a written plan for your full debt repayment. Make a written contract with yourself as to how you plan to pay each of your debts in full. Don't be discouraged. If you do not add to your debts and begin a systematic repayment plan, full repayment will happen more quickly than you might imagine. Don't be discouraged—be excited! You've taken a major step toward financial confidence.

Hint: Go to *DebtProofLiving.com* to see a demonstration of my Rapid Debt-Repayment Plan®. Members have full access to the RDRP Calculator, which is a cinch to use. Just input all of your unsecured debts, hit "Calculate" and out comes your unique re-payment plan. So easy, so simple. Quite amazing if I do say so myself! By the way, see page 225 for how you can become a member with my compliments.

Week Six:
Focus on the Future

This week it's all about future thinking. Your assignment is to make sure you have a valid and current will, a revocable living trust (if your attorney or your own independent research deter-mines this is advisable), and an advance health directive with power of attorney document signed, witnessed and put into a safe place.

Also this week it is time to explore your employer-provided retirement plan and the steps you need to take to join it. If you are already participating, review the plan to make sure you are on track. Or get busy opening an IRA or Roth IRA account with a regular monthly deposit.

You've done great and there's just one last thing you need to do today: Turn to page 225 and follow the instructions to sign up for your free membership at *DebtProofLiving.com*.

Conclusion

A Final Thought

"Hard work is worthwhile, but empty talk will make you poor."
– Proverbs 14:23

Well, our time together has just about come to a close. I don't know about you, but I'm excited! In the course of writing this book, I kept beside the keyboard a pad on which I jotted down new habits I want to learn. My own belief system has been refined and enhanced. I have a lot of work ahead of me and I'm ready to get started.

No matter what your particular calling in life right now— whether you're a wife, a mother, a professional or all three— you're a woman both wonderful and unique.

The most you need to know

You hold in your hands the least you need to know to become a financially confident woman, which begs the question: What is the most you need to know? I am so happy that question has come to your mind because there is so much. We have only touched the tip of the personal finance iceberg here.

First you need to join *DebtProofLiving.com* (please accept a three-month membership as my gift to you; see page 225). Next go to *EverydayCheapskate.com* and sign up to receive a free daily email message from me that you are going to love. This will keep us connected and you on track, taking your newly-found financial confidence to the next level.

The timing of your life, like you, is also unique. The time was right for you to read this book; the time was right for me to write it. God has wonderful plans for both of us. I pray that as you change and grow, you will embrace the new challenges that will present themselves. That those opportunities will develop excellence in your life like you've never known before.

Write to me and tell me about it. I would love to hear from you.

Mary Hunt
P.O. Box 2135
Paramount, CA 90723
mary@debtproofliving.com

Heavenly Father,

Hardly a day goes by that I'm not bombarded with tempting offers to conform to society's ideas of what I need to be happy.

Renew my mind so that I always find my contentment and security in you, not in the false security the world offers. Amen

Glossary

PITI, ARM, FICO, grace period, HELOC, Fannie Mae, Freddie Mac. Do you know what these financial terms mean? You should; and nothing will boost your financial confidence more than having a decent working knowledge of each one, plus a few others as well.

Following are the most important financial terms you need to know. Learn one a day—or week—by simply copying it to an index card or to your computer's screen saver. One important term at a time you will increase your FIQ (financial intelligence quotient). In fact, I think you're getting more confident by the minute.

Adjustable Rate Mortgage (ARM): A home loan where the interest rate is changed periodically based on a standard financial index. ARMs offer lower initial interest rates with the risk of rates increasing in the future. In comparison, a fixed rate mortgage (FRMs) offers a higher rate that will not change for the length of the loan. ARMs often have caps on how much the interest rate can rise or fall.

Alias: A note on your credit report that indicates other names used for your financial accounts. Sometimes marked as "Also Known As" or "AKA." This can include maiden names or variations on the spelling and format of your full name.

Amortization: The process of gradually repaying a debt with regularly scheduled payments.

AnnualCreditReport.com: The official website for obtaining your free credit report disclosures from the credit bureaus, Equifax, Experian and TransUnion. You have the right to request your credit reports online, by phone or by mail for free once every 12 months under FACT Act regulations. This free service can only be used once a year and does not include your credit scores or any credit monitoring services.

Annual Fee: A charge sometimes required by credit card companies for use of an account. Annual fees range between $10-50 a year and are most common with rewards cards or cards for subprime borrowers.

Annual Percentage Rate (APR): The interest rate being charged on a debt, expressed as a yearly rate. Credit cards often have several different APRs—one for purchases, one for cash advances and one for balance transfers. Some lenders may increase the APR if a payment is late.

Application Fee: Amount a lender charges to process loan application documents. Quality lenders do not charge these fees (though they may charge other fees).

Appraisal Fee: The amount charged to deliver a professional opinion about how much a property is worth. For a standard home or condominium, this fee is usually around $200-500.

Appraised Value: An educated opinion of how much a property is worth. An appraiser considers the price of similar homes in the area, the condition of the home and the features of the property to estimate the value.

Asset: Items of cash value owned by a person. These can include homes, cars, boats, savings and investments.

Average Daily Balance: This is the method that is used to calculate your credit-card interest due on the outstanding balance each month. An average daily balance is determined by adding each day's balance and then dividing that total by the number of days in a billing cycle. The average daily balance is then multiplied by a card's monthly periodic rate, which is calculated by dividing the annual percentage rate by 12. A card with an annual rate of 18 percent would have a monthly periodic rate of 1.5 percent. If that card had a $500 average daily balance it would yield a monthly finance charge of $7.50.

Authorized User: Anyone who uses your credit cards or credit accounts with your permission. More specifically, someone who has a credit card from your account with their name on it. An authorized user is not legally responsible for the debt and will not get credit score benefit from it. However, the account may appear on their credit report.

Balance Transfer: The process of moving all or part of the outstanding balance on one credit card to another account. Card issuers sometimes offer teaser rates to encourage balance transfers coming in and apply balance-transfer fees to discourage you from transferring your balance to another card.

Balloon Payment: A loan where the payments don't pay off the principal in full by the end of the term. When the loan term expires (usually after five to seven years), the borrower must pay a balloon payment for the remaining amount or refinance. Balloon loans sometimes include convertible options that allow the remaining amount to automatically be transferred into a long-term mortgage. (See Convertible ARM.)

Bankruptcy: A proceeding that legally releases a person from repaying a portion or all debts owed. Bankruptcy damages one's credit file for seven to ten years.

Beacon Score: A specific credit score developed by Equifax. There are thousands of slightly different credit scoring formulas used by bankers, lenders, creditors, insurers and retailers. Each score can vary somewhat in how it evaluates your credit data.

Bi-Weekly Mortgage: A mortgage that schedules payments every two weeks instead of the standard monthly payment. The twenty-six bi-weekly payments are each equal to one-half of a monthly payment. The result is that the mortgage is paid off sooner.

Borrower: The individual who is requesting the loan and who will be responsible to pay it back.

Cardholder: The person who is issued a credit card, and any authorized users.

Cardholder agreement: The written statement that gives the terms and conditions of a credit-card account. The cardholder agreement is required by Federal Reserve regulations. It must include the Annual Percentage Rate, the monthly minimum payment formula, annual fee if applicable, and the cardholder's rights in billing disputes. Changes in the cardholder agreement may be made, with written advance notice, at any time by the issuer. Rules for imposing changes vary from state to state, but the rules that apply are those of the home state of the issuing bank, not the home state of the cardholder.

Cash Advance: A cash loan from your creditor, usually by using your credit card at an ATM machine. Or a loan advance on your paycheck. These loans include special interest rates charged on the amount of the advance.

Cash-Advance Fee: A charge by the bank for using credit cards to obtain cash. This fee can be stated in terms of a flat per-transaction fee or a percentage of the amount of the cash advance. For example, the fee may be expressed as follows: 2 percent/$10. This means that the cash advance fee will be either 2 percent of the cash advance amount or $10, whichever is greater.

Cash-Out Refinance: A new mortgage for an existing property in which the amount borrowed is greater than the amount of the previous mortgage. The difference is given to the borrower in cash when the loan is closed.

Chapter 7 Bankruptcy: A type of consumer bankruptcy where your responsibility for your debts is cleared entirely. With this kind of bankruptcy you are not required to pay back debts you owe from before your filing. Chapter 7 bankruptcy filing records remain on your credit report for ten years and the record of each account included in your filing will remain on your report for seven years. Changes to bankruptcy law will make it more difficult to file for Chapter 7 bankruptcy in the future.

Chapter 11 Bankruptcy: A complex type of bankruptcy usually filed by businesses that wish to restructure their debts.

Chapter 13 Bankruptcy: A type of bankruptcy where the consumer must pay off some of their debts over time. Chapter 13 bankruptcy filing records remain on your credit report for seven years from the discharge date or ten years from the filing date if it is not discharged. Each account included in the filing will remain on your report for seven years.

Charge-Off: When a creditor or lender writes off the balance of a delinquent debt, no longer expecting it to be repaid. A charge-off is also known as a bad debt. Charge-off records remain on your credit report for seven years and will harm your credit score. After a debt is charged-off, it can be sold to a collections agency.

ChexSystems: A credit reporting company that tracks your banking history and provides this data to banks when you apply for a new checking account. Negative records, such as bounced checks, can be kept in their database for up to five years. If there are errors on your ChexSystems record, you can contact the company to submit a dispute.

Closing Costs: The amounts charged to a consumer when they are transferring ownership or borrowing against a property. Closing costs include lender, title and escrow fees and usually range from 3 to 6 percent of the purchase price.

Collateral: An asset or property used as security against a loan. If the borrower defaults, the lender agrees to take the collateral as payment for the loan. If the value of the collateral is not equal or greater to the outstanding amount of the loan, the borrower may be found liable for the deficient amount.

Collections: When a business sells your debt for a reduced amount to an agency in order to recover the amounts owed. Credit-card debts, medical bills, cell phone bills, utility charges, library fees and video store fees are often sold to collections. Collection agencies attempt to recover past-due debts by contacting the borrower via phone and mail. Collection records can remain on your credit report for seven years from the last 180 day late payment on the original debt. Your rights are defined by the Fair Debt Collection Practices Act.

Combined Loan-to-Value Ratio: The total amount you are borrowing in mortgage debts divided by the home's fair market value. Someone with a $50,000 first mortgage and a $20,000 equity line secured against a $100,000 house would have a CLTV ratio of 70 percent.

Commitment Fee: A fee paid by a borrower to a lender in exchange for a promise to lend money on certain terms for a specified period. Usually charged in order to extend a loan approval offer for longer than the 30-60 day standard period. Quality lenders don't usually charge these fees.

Conforming Loan: A mortgage that meets the requirements for purchase by Fannie Mae and Freddie Mac. Requirements include size of the loan, type and age. Current loan size limits for single-family homes range between $200,000 and $400,000. Loans that exceed the conforming size are considered jumbo mortgages and usually have higher interest rates.

Co-Signer: An additional person who signs a loan document and takes equal responsibility for the debt. A borrower may want to use a co-signer if their credit or financial situation is not good enough to qualify for a loan on their own. A co-signer is legally responsible for the loan and the shared account will appear on their credit report. Having a co-signer is only helpful if the co-signer's credit or financial standing is better than the primary borrower.

Convenience Checks: Checks provided by your credit card company that you can use to access your available credit. These checks often have different rates and terms than your standard credit-card charges. Frequently the terms are not printed with the checks and the only way to know what they are is to call the phone number enclosed.

Convertible ARM: An adjustable rate mortgage that can be converted to a fixed-rate mortgage under specified conditions.

CRA: Credit Reporting Agency. See Credit Bureaus.

Credit Bureaus: Also known as credit reporting agencies (CRAs), these companies collect information from creditors and lenders about consumer financial behavior. This data is then provided to businesses that want to evaluate how risky it would be to lend money to a potential borrower. Once a low-tech system of regional credit reporting agencies, the industry is now consolidated into the three national credit bureaus—Equifax, Experian and TransUnion.

Credit Counseling: A service that helps consumers repay their debts and improve their credit. Usually non-profit companies, most of these agencies offer helpful and affordable services. Consumers should be aware that there are also credit counseling agencies that are expensive, ineffective and even damaging to the client's credit (see Credit Repair). Consumers should carefully review the company's reputation and services before signing up.

Credit File: Another term for your credit report. The term *credit file* is generally used to indicate the full record of your credit history maintained by a credit bureau. Your credit report may not include all the information in your credit file.

Credit History: Another term for the information on your credit report. Your credit history is a record of how you have repaid your credit obligations in the past.

Credit Limit: The total amount that a company will allow you to charge to a credit card or credit line. It's best for your credit score to keep your credit card balances below 35 percent of your credit limit. If you spend more than your credit limit, you will be charged an over-limit penalty anywhere from $10 to $50.

Credit Obligation: An agreement where a person becomes legally responsible for paying back borrowed money.

Credit Repair: A generally unscrupulous or illegal form of credit counseling that promises the impossible, such as erasing accurate records from your credit report.

Credit Report: The individual records of a consumer's financial behavior kept by credit bureaus and provided to businesses when they want to evaluate potential borrowers. Credit reports include records on: consumer name, current and former addresses, employment, credit and loan histories, inquiries, collection records, and public records such as bankruptcy filings and tax liens. Every adult can get one free report each year from each of the big three CRAs—Experian, Equifax and TransUnion—at *AnnualCreditReport.com*.

Credit Score: A numerical evaluation of your credit history used by businesses to quickly understand how risky a borrower you are expressed as a three-digit number. Credit scores are calculated using complex mathematical formulas that look at your most current payment history, debts, credit history, inquiries and other factors from your credit report. Credit scores usually range from 300-850, with 680 or higher considered to be "good" credit scores. There are thousands of slightly different credit scoring formulas (including FICO, Beacon and Empirca scores) used by bankers, lenders, creditors, insurers and retailers. Each score can vary somewhat in how it evaluates your credit data.

Debt: The amount of money owed.

Debt Consolidation: A process of combining debts into one loan or repayment plan. Debt consolidation can be done on your own, with a financial institution or through a counseling service. Student loans are often consolidated in order to secure a lower interest rate. (See Debt Counseling and Debt Settlement.)

Debt Counseling: A type of credit counseling that focuses specifically on helping people with debt issues. Instead of consolidating debts into one loan, debt counseling agencies negotiate with your creditors using preset agreements and spread your payments over a longer period in order to reduce the monthly amount due. Usually non-profit companies, most of these agencies offer helpful and affordable services. Consumers should be aware that there are also debt counseling agencies that are expensive, ineffective and even damaging to the client's credit score (see Credit Repair).

Debt Settlement: A process where you pay an agency to negotiate directly with your creditors in the hopes of making significantly reduced settlements for your debts. Working with a debt settlement company can result in damaged credit from numerous late payments and collection records. Consumers should fully investigate the practices, reputation and costs of working with a debt settlement company before signing up, because nearly all of these companies are scams.

Debt-to-Available-Credit Ratio: The amount of money you owe in outstanding debts compared to the total amount of credit you have available though all credit cards and credit lines. This ratio measures how much of your available credit you are using. The higher your debt to available credit ratio, the more risky you appear to potential lenders.

Debt-to-Income Ratio: The percentage of your monthly pretax income that is used to pay off debts such as auto loans, student loans and credit card balances. Lenders look at two ratios: The front-end ratio is the

percentage of monthly pretax earnings that is spent on house payments. In the back-end ratio, the borrower's other debts are factored in
along with the house payments.

Default: The status of a debt account that has not been paid. Accounts
are usually listed as being in default after they have been reported late
(delinquent) several times. Defaults are a serious negative item on a
credit report.

Delinquency: A term used for late payment or lack of payment on a loan,
debt or credit-card account. Accounts are usually referred to as 30, 60,
90 or 120 days delinquent because most lenders have monthly payment cycles. Delinquencies remain on your credit report for seven years
and are damaging to your credit score.

Demand Draft Checks: A type of electronic check that can be created online by entering account numbers listed on the bottom of a personal
check and that can be cashed without a signature. This system was
originally designed to help telemarketers take check payments over the
phone. Now it is one of the fastest growing fraud tools.

Dispute: The process of submitting a request to the credit bureaus to have
an error on your credit report corrected. Disputes are investigated and
updates made to your credit report over a thirty-day period. If your correction is made, you will receive a letter from the credit bureaus and a
copy of your updated credit report. If your dispute is rejected, you will
receive a letter explaining why the credit bureau could not verify the
correction.

Empirica Score: A specific credit score developed by TransUnion. There
are thousands of slightly different credit scoring formulas used by
bankers, lenders, creditors, insurers and retailers. Each score can vary
somewhat in how it evaluates your credit data.

Equal Credit Opportunity Act (ECOA): A law that protects consumers
from discrimination on the basis of race, sex, public assistance income,
age, marital status, nationality or religion in the credit and lending
process.

Equifax: One of the three national credit bureaus (also known as credit reporting agencies) that collects and provides consumer financial records.
You can purchase your credit report from Equifax online anytime.

Equity: The fair market value of a home minus the unpaid mortgage principal and liens. You build up equity in a home as you pay down your
mortgage and as the property value increases. Also called the *lendable
value* or *net value*.

Experian: One of the three national credit bureaus that collects and provides consumer financial records. Experian (formerly known as TRW) operates the ConsumerInfo, FreeCreditReport and CreditExpert brands. You can purchase your credit report form Experian online anytime.

Expiration Term: The set number of years that a record will remain on your credit report as mandated by the FCRA. Most negative records stay on your credit report for seven to ten years. The shortest expiration term is two years for inquiry records. The longest expiration term is fifteen years for paid tax liens or indefinitely for unpaid tax liens. Positive information can also stay on your credit report indefinitely.

Fair and Accurate Credit Transaction (FACT) Act: The FACT Act was signed into law December 2003 and includes several consumer credit industry regulations. This law requires credit bureaus to provide all US residents with a free copy of their credit report once every twelve months. The law also includes new privacy regulations, identity theft protections and dispute procedure requirements.

Fair Credit Reporting Act (FCRA): A federal law first passed in the 1970's that promotes accuracy, confidentiality and proper use of information in the files kept by credit reporting agencies. This law specifies the expiration terms of records on your credit report, defines who can access your credit data and grants consumers the right to view and dispute their credit records. This act is available online at *FTC.gov*.

Fannie Mae: The largest mortgage investor. A government-sponsored enterprise that buys mortgages from lenders, bundles them into investments and sells them on the secondary mortgage market. Formerly known as the Federal National Mortgage Association.

Federal Housing Administration (FHA): A division of the Department of Housing and Urban Development (HUD) that provides mortgage insurance and sets construction and underwriting standards.

FICO Score: A specific credit score developed by Fair Isaac Corporation. There are thousands of slightly different credit scoring formulas used by bankers, lenders, creditors, insurers and retailers. Each score can vary somewhat in how it evaluates your credit data.

File Freeze: Residents of select states (currently California, Louisiana, Texas, Vermont and Washington) can request that the credit bureaus freeze their credit reports. This freeze stops new credit from being issued in your name by blocking creditors, lenders, insurers and other companies from accessing your credit data. In some cases, a $10 fee for each credit bureau is required to process the file freeze. The freeze can also be temporarily or permanently undone for an additional fee.

Finance Charge: The total cost of using credit. Besides interest charges, the finance charge may include other costs, such as cash-advance fees.

First Mortgage: The primary loan on a real estate property. This loan has priority over all other "secondary" loans.

Fixed Rate: An interest rate for a credit card or loan that remains constant.

Fixed-Rate Option: A home equity line of credit financing option that allows borrowers to specify the payments and interest on a portion of their balance. This can be done a few times during the life of the loan, usually for an additional fee.

Fixed Rate Mortgage (FRM): A mortgage with an interest rate that remains constant for the entire duration of the loan. FRM's have longer terms (fifteen to thirty years) and higher interest rates than adjustable rate mortgages but are not at risk for changing interest rates.

Foreclosure: When a borrower is in default on a loan or mortgage, the creditor can enact a legal process to claim ownership of the collateral property. Foreclosure usually involves a forced sale of the property where the proceeds go toward paying off the debt.

Fraud Alert: If you suspect that you are a victim of identity theft, you may contact the credit bureaus to request that a ninety-day fraud alert is placed on your credit reports. This alert notifies potential creditors to take extra steps to verify your identity before opening a new account. If you have been a victim of identity theft you only need to contact one bureau to have a temporary ninety-day alert added to all three of your credit reports. This ninety-day alert notifies potential creditors that your identity may have been stolen and suggests that they take extra steps to confirm your identity before opening a new account. If it turns out that your identity has been stolen, you can request an extended seven-year alert by providing documentation of the crime (such as a police report). There is also a special one-year fraud alert available for military personnel on activity duty.

Freddie Mac: Formerly known as the Federal Home Loan Mortgage Corporation, this is a government-sponsored firm that buys mortgages from lenders, pools them with other loans and sells them to investors.

Front-End Ratio or Front Ratio: A calculation of the percentage of your monthly pretax income that goes toward a house payment. The general rule is that your front ratio shouldn't exceed 28 percent.

Garnishment: When a creditor receives legal permission to take a portion of your assets (bank account, salary, etc.) to repay a delinquent debt.

Ginnie Mae: Also known as the Government National Mortgage Association. A part of the Department of Housing and Urban Development that buys mortgages from lending institutions and pools them to form securities, which it then sells to investors.

Grace Period: A period of time, often about 25 days, during which you can pay your credit-card bill without incurring a finance charge. With most credit-card accounts, the grace period applies only if you pay your balance in full each month. It does not apply if you carry a balance forward or in the case of cash advances. If your account has no grace period, interest will be charged on a purchase as soon as it is made.

High-LTV Equity Loan: A specific kind of home loan that causes your loan-to-value ratio to be 125 percent or more. When the total principal of a loan leaves the borrower with debt that exceeds the fair market value of the home, the interest paid on the portion of the loan above that value may not be tax deductible.

Home Equity Line of Credit (HELOC): An open-ended loan that is backed by the part of a home's value that the borrower owns outright. This type of loan is used much like a credit card. Home equity lines of credit can be effective ways to borrow large sums of money with a relatively low interest rate. These types of loans should be used with caution. If a borrower is unable to pay back the loan for some reason (loss of job, illness, etc.) they risk losing the home they used as collateral.

Home Equity: The part of a home's value that the mortgage borrower owns outright. This is the difference between the fair market value of the home and the principal balances of all mortgage loans.

Home Equity Loan (HEL): A loan that is backed by part of a home's equity. The entire amount is received by the borrower in a single payout with interest paid monthly on the outstanding balance (unlike a HELOC where the borrower draws on the amount approved, as needed, and pays interest only on the amount drawn).

Home Ownership and Equity Protection Act: A law designed to discourage predatory lending in mortgages and home equity loans.

Housing Expense Ratio: The percentage of your monthly pretax income that goes toward your house payment. The general rule is that this ratio shouldn't exceed 28 percent. This is also known as the "front ratio."

Income Verification: Loan applications may require fully documented proof of an applicant's income. Loans of this type usually offer lower interest rates than no-income or "no-doc" verification loans.

Inquiry: An item on your credit report that shows that someone with a "permissible purpose" under FCRA regulations has previously requested a copy of your credit report data. (See Soft Inquiry and Promotional Inquiry.)

Installment Account: A type of loan where the borrower makes the same payment each month. This includes personal loans and automobile loans. Mortgage loans are also installment accounts but are usually classified by the credit reporting system as real-estate accounts instead.

Interest Rate Cap: A limit on how much a borrower's percentage rate can increase or decrease at rate adjustment periods and over the life of the loan. Interest rate caps are used for ARM loans where the rates can vary at certain points.

Interest Rate: A measure of the cost of credit, expressed as a percent. For variable-rate credit card-plans, the interest rate is explicitly tied to another interest rate. The interest rate on fixed-rate credit card plans, though not explicitly tied to changes in other interest rates, can also change over time.

Interest: The money a borrower pays for the ability to borrow from a lender or creditor. Interest is calculated as a percentage of the money borrowed and is paid over a specified time.

Interest-Only Loan: A type of loan where the repayment only covers the interest that accumulates on the loan balance and not the actual price of the property. The principal does not decrease with the payments. Interest-only loans usually have a term of one to five years, after which the entire principal becomes due and payable.

Introductory Rate: A temporary, low interest rate offered on a credit card in order to attract customers. This low rate usually lasts for about six months before converting to a normal fixed or variable rate. With some offers, the introductory rate can be revoked or terminated early if you make a late payment or violate some other terms of the account.

Joint Account: An account shared by two or more people. Each person on the account is legally responsible for the debt and the account will be reported to each person's credit report.

Judgment: A decision from a judge on a civil action or lawsuit; usually an amount of money a person is required to pay to satisfy a debt or as a penalty. Judgment records remain on your credit report for seven years and harm your credit score significantly.

Jumbo Mortgage: A loan that exceeds the limits set by Fannie Mae and Freddie Mac (usually when the loan amount is more than $200,000-400,000). Also known as a non-conventional or non-conforming loan, these mortgages usually have higher interest rates than standard loans.

Late Payment: A delinquent payment or failure to deliver a loan or debt payment on or before the time agreed. Late payments harm your credit score for up to seven years and are usually penalized with late payment charges.

Late Payment Charge: A fee charged by your creditor or lender when your credit-card payment is made after the date due. Late payment charges typically run from $25-$50 per occurrence, regardless the amount owed. Late fees on mortgages and installment loans are typically less harsh than open-ended accounts.

Lender: The individual or financial institution who will be providing the loan.

Lien: A legal claim against a person's property, such as a car or a house, as security for a debt. A lien (pronounced "lean") may be placed by a contractor who did work on your house or a mechanic who repaired your car and didn't get paid. The property cannot be sold without pay-ing the lien. Tax liens can remain on your credit report indefinitely if left unpaid, or for fifteen years from the date paid.

Loan Origination Fee: A fee charged by a lender for underwriting a loan. The fee often is expressed in "points;" a point is 1 percent of the loan amount.

Loan Processing Fee: A fee charged by a lender for accepting a loan appli-cation and gathering the supporting paperwork, usually about $300.

Loan-to-Value Ratio (LTV): The percentage of a home's price that is fi-nanced with a loan. On a $100,000 house, if the buyer makes a $20,000 down payment and borrows $80,000, the loan-to-value ratio is 80 percent. When refinancing a mortgage, the LTV ratio is calculated using the appraised value of the home, not the sale price. You will usu-ally get the best deal if your LTV ratio is below 80 percent.

Low-Documentation Loan: A mortgage that requires less income and or assets verification than a conventional loan. Low-documentation loans are designed for entrepreneurs or self-employed borrowers—or for borrowers who cannot or choose not to reveal information about their incomes.

Low-Down Mortgages: Secured loans that require a small down payment, usually less than 10 percent. Often, low-down mortgages are offered to special kinds of borrowers such as first-time buyers, police officers, veterans, etc. These kinds of loans sometimes require that mortgage insurance is purchased by the borrower.

Maxed Out: A slang term for using up the entire credit limit on a credit card or a line of credit. Borrowing the maximum limit on cards or equity lines hurts your credit score.

Merged Credit Report: Also called a 3-in-1 Credit Report, this type of report shows your credit data from TransUnion, Equifax and Experian in a side-by-side format for easy comparison. You will pay a fee to get this. Free reports required by law are available only at *AnnualCredit Report.com.*

Minimum Payment: The minimum amount that a credit card company requires you to pay toward your debt each month, usually 3 to 4 percent of the outstanding balance or not less than $10.

Mortgage Banker: A person or company that originates home loans, sells them to investors and processes monthly payments.

Mortgage Broker: A person or company that matches lenders with borrowers who meet their criteria. A mortgage broker does not make the loan directly like a mortgage banker, but receives payment for their services.

Mortgage Refinance: The process of paying off and replacing an old loan with a new mortgage. Borrowers usually choose to refinance a mortgage to get a lower interest rate, lower their monthly payments, avoid a balloon payment or to take cash out of their equity.

Mutual Fund: Also called a "stock mutual fund," this is simply a fund that owns dozens, if not hundreds, of individual stocks. A mutual fund gives you instant diversification: You buy shares of a mutual fund, and each share gives you a stake in all the different stocks owned by the fund.

Negative Amortization: This occurs when your minimum payment toward a debt is not enough to cover the interest charges. Your debt balance continues to increase despite your payments.

No-Documentation Loan: Also called a "stated income" mortgage in which the applicant provides only the minimum information—name, address and Social Security number. The underwriter decides on the loan based only on the applicant's credit history, the appraised value of the house and size of down payment. This type of loan usually has higher interest rates than a standard loan. Subprime mortgages are often stated-income loans.

Opt-Out: You can opt-out from pre-approved credit card offers, insurance offers and other third party marketing by calling 888-5-OPT-OUT. Calling this number will stop mail offers that use your credit data from all three credit bureaus. You can also call this number to ask to opt-in again.

Over-Limit Fee: A fee charged by a creditor when your spending exceeds the credit limit set on your card, usually $10 to $50.

Penalty Rate: Also called "default rate," a higher interest rate applied to your credit-card account if you are late making payments.

Periodic Rate: The interest rate you are charged each billing period. For most credit cards, the periodic rate is a monthly rate. You can calculate your card's periodic rate by dividing the APR by twelve. A credit card with an 18-percent APR has a monthly periodic rate of 1.5 percent.

PITI: Acronym for the four elements of a mortgage payment: principal, interest, taxes and insurance.

Point: A unit for measuring fees related to a loan; a point equals 1 percent of a mortgage loan. Some lenders charge "origination points" to cover the expense of making a loan. Some borrowers pay "discount points" to reduce the loan's interest rate.

Pre-approved: A credit card offer with "pre-approved" only means that a potential customer has passed a preliminary credit-information screening. A credit card company can spurn the customers it invited with "pre-approved" junk mail if it doesn't like the applicant's credit rating.

Pre-Approval Letter: A document from a lender or broker that estimates how much a potential homebuyer could borrow based on current interest rates and a preliminary look at credit history. The letter is a not a binding agreement with a lender. Having a pre-approval letter can make it easier to shop for a home and negotiate with sellers. It is better to have a pre-approval letter than an informal pre-qualification letter.

Prepayment Penalty: A fee that a lender charges a borrower who pays off the loan before the end of its scheduled term. Prepayment penalties are not charged by most standard lenders. Subprime borrowers should review the terms of their loan offers carefully to see if this fee is included.

Principal: The amount of money borrowed with a loan or the amount of money owed, excluding interest.

Private Mortgage Insurance (PMI): A form of insurance that protects the lender by paying the costs of foreclosing on a house if the borrower stops paying the loan. Private mortgage insurance usually is required if the down payment is less than 20 percent of the sale price.

Promotional Inquiry: A type of soft inquiry made by a creditor, lender or insurer in order to send you a pre-approved offer. Only limited credit data is made available for this type of inquiry and it does not harm your credit score.

Public Records: Information that is available to any member of the public. Public records like a bankruptcy, tax lien, foreclosure, court judgment or overdue child support harm your credit report and credit score significantly.

Qualifying Ratios: As calculated by lenders, the percentage of income that is spent on housing debt and combined household debt.

Rate Shopping: Applying for credit with several lenders to find the best interest rate, usually for a mortgage or a car loan. If done within a short period of time, such as two weeks, it should have little impact on a person's credit score.

Re-aging Accounts: A process where a creditor can roll-back an account record with the credit bureaus. This is commonly used when cardholders request that late payment records are removed because they are incorrect or resulting from a special circumstance. However, re-aging can also be used illegally by collections agencies to make a debt account appear much younger than it actually is. Some collections agencies use this tactic to keep an account from expiring from your credit report in order to try to get you to pay the debt.

Repayment Period: The period of a loan when a borrower is required to make payments. It usually applies to home equity lines of credit. During the repayment period, the borrower cannot take out any more money and must pay down the loan.

Repossession: When a loan is significantly overdue, a creditor can claim property (cars, boats, equipment, etc.) that was used as collateral for the debt.

Reverse Mortgage: A mortgage that allows elderly borrowers to access their equity without selling their home. The lender makes payments to the borrower with a reverse mortgage. The loan is repaid from the proceeds of the estate when the borrower moves or passes away.

Revolving Account: An account where your balance and monthly payment can fluctuate. Most credit cards are revolving accounts.

Rewards Card: A credit card that rewards spending with points, cash back programs or airline miles. These types of cards usually require that borrowers have good credit and commonly involve an annual fee.

Risk Score: Another term for a credit score. (See Credit Score, FICO Score, Beacon Score and Empirica Score.)

Schumer Box: An easy-to-use chart that explains the rates, fees, terms and conditions of a credit account. Creditors are required to provide this on credit applications by the U.S. Truth in Lending Act, and it usually appears on statements and other documents.

Scoring Model: A complex mathematical formula that evaluates financial data to predict a borrower's future behavior. Developed by the credit bureaus, banks and FICO, there are thousands of slightly different scoring models used to generate credit scores.

Second Mortgage: A loan using a home's equity as collateral. A first mortgage must be repaid before a second mortgage in a sale.

Secured Credit Card: A consumer credit account that requires the borrower to produce some form of collateral—usually a cash deposit equal to the amount of the credit limit on the card. Secured credit cards are easier to obtain than standard credit accounts and are helpful for borrowers with poor credit or no credit.

Secured Debt: A loan that requires a piece of property (such as a house or car) to be used as collateral. This collateral provides security for the lender, since the property can be seized and sold if you don't repay the debt.

Settlement: An agreement reached with a creditor to pay a debt for less than the total amount due. Settlements can be noted on your credit report and are not as beneficial to your credit as paying a debt in full.

Social Security Number: Also referred to as a SSN. This unique nine digit number is meant to track your Social Security savings but is also used by creditors, lenders, banks, insurers, hospitals, employers and numerous other businesses to identify your accounts. People who do not have a SSN, such as non-US citizens, use a nine digit Individual Taxpayer Identification Number (ITIN) instead.

Soft Inquiry: A type of inquiry that does not harm your credit score. Soft inquires are recorded when a business accesses your credit data for a purpose other than an application for credit. Soft inquiries include your request to see your own credit report and employment-related requests. This type of inquiry is recorded by the credit bureaus but does not usually appear on a credit report purchased by you or a business.

Stock: A share of ownership in a company. Owners of stock receive part of the company's profits—and bear some of its losses—up to the amount of money they put into the stock.

Subprime Borrower: A borrower who does not meet the qualifications for standard credit and loan offers. Usually a subprime borrower has poor credit (a score under 650) due to late payments, collection accounts or public records. Subprime borrowers can qualify for loans and credit, but usually at a higher interest rate or with special terms.

Teaser rate: Often called the introductory rate, it is the below-market interest rate offered to entice customers to switch credit cards or lenders.

TransUnion: One of the three national credit bureaus that collects and provides consumer financial records. TransUnion operates the TrueCredit and FreeCreditProfile brands.

TRW: A former credit reporting agency that is now part of Experian.

Universal Default Clause: A credit card policy that allows a creditor to increase your interest rates if you make a late payment on any account, not just on their account. For example, your rates could increase dramatically on your credit card if you make a late payment on an unrelated loan. Your creditors track your payment history with other accounts by checking your credit report. Some credit card issuers now advertise they have voluntarily ceased to exercise their rights to universal default.

Unsecured Debt: A loan on which there is no collateral. Most credit-card accounts are unsecured debt.

Utilization Ratio: The ratio between the credit limits on your accounts and the outstanding balances. This ratio shows lenders how much of your available credit you are using overall.

Variable Rate: A type of adjustable rate loan tied directly to the movement of some other economic index. For example, a variable rate might be prime rate plus 3 percent; it will adjust as the prime rate does.

Index